ALMANAC

PRAISE FOR *ALMANAC*

"In *Almanac*, Christine Gelineau draws from a particular life, her own, different than mine or yours, but the differences fade to the margins of consciousness in the deeply felt connection she establishes with the reader. It's a connection based on her fidelity to what is, to the real feel of our living. She helps us hear the heartbeat under the noise, hers and ours. And the heartbeat of the horses that have accompanied her on her journey. Her love of horses opens on a love of the world and is the source of the many beauties of this book, and of the profound solace it provides."

— Kevin Oderman, author of *How Things Fit Together: Fifteen Essays*, winner of the Bakeless Prize in Nonfiction

"I read Christine Gelineau's *Almanac* at a single sitting, enthralled by a book at once so capacious and so grounded, so intimate and so wise. Gelineau gets that 'history—personal, national, global, cosmic—is an artifact' made of language, and she registers history here at all those scales in finely honed, pitch-perfect language, but she also recognizes that nature 'is outside of language, ineluctably real,' and the birth of a foal in a cold April barn is as present here as challenges in her childhood and the colonial complications of the Americas and emergency brain surgery and climate catastrophe. Horses and humans alike take pleasure, Gelineau observes, in the 'sensation of meaning and order.' Art, she says, can offer that sensation. Her book, I say, does offer it."

— H. L. Hix, author of over thirty books, including *Chromatic*, a finalist for the National Book Award

Almanac
A MURMURATION

Christine Gelineau

excelsior editions

Photo credit for interior photographs: Christine Gelineau. The photos were taken on the author's farm, with the singular exception of the "January" photo, which depicts Taughannock Falls in Ulysses, New York.

Cover Credit: Shutterstock.
Published by State University of New York Press, Albany
© 2025 State University of New York
All rights reserved
Printed in the United States of America

No part of this book may be used or reproduced in any manner whatsoever without written permission. No part of this book may be stored in a retrieval system or transmitted in any form or by any means including electronic, electrostatic, magnetic tape, mechanical, photocopying, recording, or otherwise without the prior permission in writing of the publisher.

Links to third-party websites are provided as a convenience and for informational purposes only. They do not constitute an endorsement or an approval of any of the products, services, or opinions of the organization, companies, or individuals. SUNY Press bears no responsibility for the accuracy, legality, or content of a URL, the external website, or for that of subsequent websites.

EU GPSR Authorised Representative:

Logos Europe, 9 rue Nicolas Poussin, 17000, La Rochelle, France
contact@logoseurope.eu

Excelsior Editions is an imprint of State University of New York Press
For information, contact State University of New York Press, Albany, NY
www.sunypress.edu

Library of Congress Cataloging-in-Publication Data

Names: Gelineau, Christine, author.
Title: Almanac : a murmuration / Christine Gelineau.
Description: Albany : State University of New York Press, 2025. | Series:
 Excelsior editions
Identifiers: LCCN 2024039367 | ISBN 9798855801798 (paperback) | ISBN
 9798855801781 (ebook)
Subjects: LCSH: Gelineau, Christine. | Authors, American—20th century—Biography.
Classification: LCC PS3607.E44 Z46 2025 | DDC 813/.6 [B]—dc23/eng/20240828
LC record available at https://lccn.loc.gov/2024039367

This book is dedicated to all of my beloveds. I know that just as my love for them suffuses my life, it permeates as well all the pages here, even when that presence is not overtly apparent to the reader.

CONTENTS

ACKNOWLEDGMENTS	IX
January	1
February	9
March	19
April	33
May	47
June	57
July	67
August	79
September	97
October	115
November	127
December	139
WORKS CITED	153

ACKNOWLEDGMENTS

Thanks to Richard Carlin, Jenn Bennett-Genthner, Caitlin Bean, Laura Glenn, Kate Seburyamo, Michelle Alamillo, Julia Cosacchi, and the full team at SUNY Press. Thanks to my early listeners/readers Nancy McKinley, Beverly Donofrio, Catharine Foote, Margaret Sise, and Stephen Herz; to Janine Gelineau for her help and expertise in formatting the photographs properly; and to Courtney Herz, Jon Dunlap, and Jillian Dunlap for technical help and support when needed. Sincere thanks to my family, friends, colleagues, and students who contributed in ways large and small. As always, thanks to Stephen.

Thanks also due to Leslie Jill Patterson, Donna Baier Stein, and Neil Shepard, the editors of these journals who published the following portions of what became this book: "April," first section, is excerpted from my essay, "Foal Watch," which was published in *Iron Horse Literary Review* IV, no. 2 (Spring 2003); "June," section 2, a few lines included in June #8, and June #9, are excerpted from "Finding My Own Way to the Garden," originally published in *Tiferet* (Summer 2017); "August," section 5 and "September," section 10 are excerpted from "Meditation on a Brush Pile," which appeared in *Plant-Human Quarterly* 7 (Winter Solstice 2022); "May," section 1 and "June," section 1 have been published in *Plant-Human Quarterly* 12 (Spring Equinox 2024), where they appear lineated under the titles "May" and "Communion."

January

Here in the American Northeast the new year opens with shattering cold, saltwater coves frozen over and ocean waves slurred to slush, while Niagara Falls grows hoodoos of ice, a landscape as glittering and dangerous as the human imagination.

The roll of the year aligns with perigee — that period when the moon is at the point of its orbit closest to earth — which, in turn has aligned with the full-moon phase, a syzygy of effects we refer to as a supermoon. The supermoon floats in the silvered sky, it tugs at the slurried waves.

This long, frigid night is lit and warmed by that moon's encompassing presence, the serenity of its disc of light suggestive, but austere.

Released from their stalls in the crisp first new year's morning, the horses care nothing for our calculations, our count that divides yesterday from today irrelevant to their concerns: even our calibrations of the cold — eight below — they absorb without abstraction, the snow crying out beneath their hooves as they home in on the heaped-up hay we've spread for them on the snow's clean plate.

It's cold you need to push against, lean into as you walk, but no wind bites: new year's wish enough for horses, their happy hopes for the morning fulfilled by sweet dried grass and the freedom to loaf together beneath the chill, white sun.

My mother didn't take any crap. Except the crap she doled out to herself. Already I've written two things my mother would not have approved of: the word *crap*, and a lead-in that suggests I'm about to air her dirty laundry. "It's not anyone else's business," she would say.

My mother's father had been raised in a small town in County Tyrone, Ireland, an area currently designated as part of Northern Ireland, her mother on a rocky, thin-soiled farm in a miniscule settlement in County Galway, next to Rossaveel, where the ferry for the Aran Islands docks, her mother tongue Irish, his English.

These are the kinds of communities in which everyone knows everyone else's business and you live together with your intimate knowledge of one another's business not only for the whole of your life, but for generation after generation. You know not just your neighbor's secrets but the secrets of their siblings, their parents, their parents' parents, and they know the same of you. It can breed in a deeply held sense of secrecy.

Ireland is a nation of singers and storytellers who keep their personal stories close. Who practice deflection, indirection.

Americans, by contrast, are bred to pastlessness, reinvention, and these days to oversharing and display.

I have an early memory of my family out for a Sunday drive — that was a thing then, a Sunday drive. I'll come back to my mother soon, but for now I'm remembering my father pulling the car to the side of the road so Christine could see the horses grazing in the pasture. Occasionally he even brought me out of the car to stand by the fence, feel the sun and the rough wooden boards, smell the meadow grasses, and watch the pacific horses crop, while my mother and siblings waited in the car.

In the earliest of these memories, I must have been no more than four. How had I even discovered for myself, or communicated to my parents, this unaccountable obsession of a little girl growing up on a quarter-acre lot in the Rhode Island suburbs? Under what circumstances had I even encountered a horse in order to fall in love?

My parents presumed they were indulging a phase.

Could Pegasus, the wingéd horse of Greek mythology, have been the spark of my horse fixation? Scarlet, electric. Alphabet, mythology, pattern.

Our house was the first one as you turned into Oak Hill Terrace, the realtor-speak moniker the developer had given to the cluster of houses — colonial, ranch, Cape, colonial, ranch, Cape — he had planted in the scraped-bare lots after he leveled the oaks that had once been on that hill. Then he dotted each small lot with spindly saplings, mostly maple. We neighborhood kids called our turf, *the plat*, to my mother's dismay, since that word — even onomatopoetically — so thoroughly undermined the aspirational lilt of the official name.

Our yard at the edge of the plat bordered commercial lots on busy Oaklawn Avenue. All fourteen of the years I lived there, the lot beside us was undeveloped. Next to that overgrown field, and abutting our backyard, was the lot for Superior Bakery and across Oaklawn from Superior, was the ESSO gas station, ESSO being the earlier incarnation of what we now call Exxon.

Exxon's crimson Pegasus originated as a corporate trademark with a subsidiary company in South Africa in 1911, and was trademarked in the US by Mobil Oil in the 1930s. Though the Greeks had associated their Pegasus with divine inspiration and poetry, no doubt for the oil company the idea was more along the lines of, "Drive a car — like your horse, with wings."

Not that any of that was in the mind of the toddler in the upstairs back bedroom of that first house on Rose Hill Drive, the little girl tucked under the covers of her first big-girl bed, while baby brother, Kevin, slept in the crib.

The Little Red Bed, the youth bed that would fit in with the crib in that tiny room, was snugged up to the window at the back of the house, the lights of the businesses on Oaklawn Avenue my first constellations.

Lying there in bed each night, I watched letters forming in the dark: E-S-S-O. As soon as the O was reached, the whole would imprint in neon on the parchment of the night sky: ESSO, and hold. Repeat. Did neon Pegasus wink with the letters, or hold steady in the sky? My memory is it blinked out for one beat just as ESSO was ready to appear entire.

Certainly neither of my parents ever said the word *Pegasus* — or for that matter, *poetry* — to me. Either may at one time or another have seen me looking out the window at the sign and said the word *horse*. Then either would have snapped down the Venetian blinds and told me to go to sleep.

But there within easy reach of the window, their obedient firstborn daughter instead cracked the slats of the blinds to see that lollipop-red beacon signaling to her: E-S-S-O ESSO E-S-S-O ESSO, the reassuring pattern, the ascendant wingéd horse mounting the dark, horses and poetry flickering into my childhood dreams.

There are landscapes that imprinted early and shaped my sense of the solace the world could offer me: Breakheart Pond in Rhode Island's Arcadia State Park, with inlets choked by the pulpy pads and luminescent petals of wild waterlilies; the wooded bridle paths of Goddard Park with Narragansett Bay glinting through the tree trunks; Beavertail — the tide pools and astringent granite slabs aslant on the point of Conanicut Island in that same bay; the Ocean Path at Acadia National Park in Maine. The Spit at Popponesset in Mashpee, Massachusetts on Cape Cod.

Elizabeth Bishop has a wonderful poem called "In the Waiting Room," in which she palpably enacts the experience of a young child recognizing her own human "selfness": "You are an *I*, / You are an *Elizabeth*," she is astonished, and more than a little appalled to realize.

A not insignificant portion of my own grasp of this revelatory discovery of selfness, of inexplicable and inextricable embeddness in humanity and mortality, I associate with the Spit at Popponesset — walking its length with my cousin Donna, that long strand of open beach, crossed by tanklike, prehistoric horseshoe crabs, and pierced by the cries and swoops of nesting terns, gulls, and piping plovers — or waking before dawn with my father and my older brother Gibby to walk to the cove at low tide, quahog rakes and buckets in hand. Waiting for more light, bare feet in the primordial ooze, the sucking lap of the dark salt water around our shins, pale light turning to pastel, to petal pink, the sky, the sea, the exposed sand bed of the cove pocked with air holes, the tiny spoutings of the buried quahogs — their own respiration inadvertently betraying their hiding places — immersed then in both remorseless vulnerability and heartbreaking beauty, both merging, and emerging, composite, and alone.

❖

My mother's parents were literate, but marginally so. Gramps' schooling had been the equivalent of, say, third grade, while my Nana had managed maybe a year more, on the days when she could afford the brick of peat that was her tuition. My grandfather hurriedly left Aughnacloy at the age of sixteen, seventeen, while farther south and west, on a little peninsula that crooked its rocky finger into Galway Bay, my grandmother, younger still, left behind the ten-foot-by-sixteen-foot loose stone cottage that was home to a family of nine, making room for the wee ones by shipping out for America.

Feeling sharply the lack of their own education, my grandparents had taken special pride in seeing to it that all their children had the chance at high school, even the oldest, my mother. As the eldest, my mother had used her good grades to graduate, without ceremony, in January of her senior year so she could find work and help support the family. Though she would have been in the running for valedictorian had she been able to stay, those kinds of extras were a frivolity she could not afford. By June and time for caps and gowns, she was already traveling to her job in Boston and taking evening classes at a secretarial school.

Seventeen years old and fresh out of high school, my mother found work in nearby Boston, though she lived at home in Needham. Her father would never have consented to her living on her own, and besides, an apartment would have been a waste of money when she already had a room to share with her sister Norine, and her income could help to stretch the family finances. But away from home she was different, freer, wholly American. She made friends, bought smart clothes with her own earnings. She became a sophisticate. A young, pretty, single girl in Boston.

❖

Though she didn't pass that set of physical characteristics on to a single one of her children, Marion Coyle was Black Irish. She had the astonishing coloration of her Galway heritage: a fair Irish complexion the color of cream roses and intensely green eyes, but the glossy black hair that is traditionally believed to be the legacy of Spanish sailors who put to port in Galway. So richly black and shining was my mother's hair, strangers would lean over on the bus and ask to touch it. Ritualistically after she washed it, my mother would rub her hair in the towel, polishing the strands together to bring out the luster.

My mother completed her high school requirements in 1941, so the beaus who courted her in her late teens and early twenties were men in uniform for whom one had to wait. Among those suitors, one in particular stood out as special and as the war wound down at last, their imminent engagement began to be presumed.

Was it the summer of 1945? Could the twenty-one-year-old who would one day be my mother be sitting on the sand on Cape Cod with her girlfriends vacationing while the mushroom cloud bloomed over Hiroshima, the city and its inhabitants vaporized?

The taste of war's end was in the air here on the home front, a giddy element of relief. Marion met some new friends on that trip, in particular a young woman from Rhode Island whose three older brothers had all survived the infantry intact and would soon be coming home from Europe.

Certainly Marion was serious about her young man, but she wasn't *actually* engaged. His picture was tucked in her wallet as she took the train from Boston down to Providence to visit with Eva Gelineau that autumn day. Marion's suit was camel's hair, trimmed with a fur collar. Not actually mink, but thick, mink-dark and stylish nonetheless. A band of matching fur held back the soft curls of her glossy hair, her high heels, bag, and gloves in deep brown leather coordinated pleasingly. The seams of her stockings slid neatly up the backs of her legs, her nails were manicured, lipstick carefully applied. She stepped from the train there in Providence into the gold wash of an Indian summer afternoon.

Eva's brother Gilbert had mustered out of the Army only days before. End-of-the-war slim, rakishly mustachioed, buoyant with being young and alive and home. His eyes were so blue the color was startling. I don't know if he suspected machinations on his sister's part when Eva suggested he meet her friend at the train station, but I do know it was meteorology when they met. The confidently smiling young man on the photograph in her purse didn't have a chance.

Slung in the slow swing of the galaxy's cradle, Earth rolls its inconsequential head: an infant who understands his own head turn as his mother's disappearance.

The Milky Way's powdered rim appears to Earth to tilt: a gunwale of stars across which we gaze.

❖

During the Second World War, the US government used Popponesset Beach and Popponesset Island for amphibious training exercises. By what wartime powers of eminent domain were the lands acquired by the government and from exactly whom? What I do know is that in the early 1950s, the government deactivated the camp and sold off its holdings at Popponesset Beach. The one-time government installation became the start of a little beach community of cottages owned by working class to scrambling-into-the-middle-class people from Boston. I have no doubt but that blacks were redlined from being included in this opportunity but my factory-worker grandparents, who had faced No Irish Need Apply signs in their own work lives, were nevertheless able to buy what had been the mess hall, and my godparents — my Aunt Norine and Uncle Sandy — bought one of the new little cottages on the far corner of the grid of sand roads that was the original Popponesset Beach Association.

How did factory workers buy a second home, walking distance from the sea? The coast had not yet been developed as it is now, and their cottages needed to pay their own way. Most of the season was rented out. These days there's a whole industry in America's seaside communities of property upkeep: handymen, landscapers, and cleaners. In the 1950s, in my family, my grandparents, and typically my uncle, would fight the traffic down to the Cape, clean and repair between renters, and drive back home, reserving only two weeks or so for themselves to begin with, but gradually one could pay off the mortgage, keep a few trusted returning renters for enough weeks out of the season to pay the taxes.

When I was four, my brother entered first grade. Gibby brought his reader home from school and we sat together on the living room couch, my legs not yet even reaching to the end of the seat cushions. What second-born isn't an acolyte to the firstborn at that age and reading was the most fascinating thing I had ever witnessed my brother doing. The trick of decoding the alphabet and then combining and recombining those twenty-six distinctive marks to conjure up words — the miracle of encoding speech and thought in sign that endured, could be stored and transported, the way ideas and information could transfer between persons and across time and space. My apprehension of the magic of that has never faded. By the time I went to first grade myself, I had been reading for two years. My first day of first grade, I carried my reading book home with me and read it cover to cover. I can still remember my disappointment the next day when I realized the book was intended to last us the year, not the evening.

My elementary school years were spent at St. Joseph's School in the neighboring town of West Warwick. Still a mission church of a parish in Montreal, the congregation and student population at St. Joseph's was noticeably weighted toward French Canadians, while on the opposing corner of the intersection was Sacred Heart, a second Catholic church and school, that one full of Italian-American children. A certain tribalism by ethnicity was baked into my early understandings of the nature of the human community.

If nature tutors us, the lesson is: nature will be nature. She will go on in strict obedience to natural laws, the laws we've spent centuries manipulating from the depths of the pit of our unintended consequences, the maw of what we do not know, and what we know but have done nothing about.

Nature will not save us from ourselves.

This January frozen sharks have washed ashore in Massachusetts, and the swamps of North Carolina snapped shut in the cold, ice ringed around the trees, the reeds, the stilled snouts of alligators.

February

Nightlong the noiseless snow drops with relentless patience, storming with persistence not ferocity. In its wake, I wade out with my shovel, releasing our domestic byways from the marble of the snow the way the sculptor released his figures from the stone, dis-covering, re-membering the buried pathways, a concrete representation of the insight that to recall is inevitably an act of re-vision, of re-configuration, reinvention.

It takes the whole of your body leaning into the effort to wrestle the massive sliding door shut against February, sealing up the sheltering hive of the barn.

Should the roof and soffits be under assault by an icy sleet or brutish wind, you may find the horses waiting with a measure of contentment but in a silent piling up of snow like this one, the impatience and expectation are palpable even as you snug the door closed.

Horses are not meant for confinement. They are not opposed to stalls in the proper measure — our horses divide their days between in and out and are happy enough for a secure corner in the winter darkness, or a shady retreat in the insect-heavy summer sun. Horses are herd animals, almost without exception preferring to be among others of their kind over being alone, while at the same time they are primal as middle schoolers about the hierarchy of the group so the screen-topped stalls keep everyone in sight of one another, but provide each their own space, their own hay supply, water source, and undisturbed nest of bedding to drowse on. But come morning in winter or evening in summer, the horses remember their feral souls, remember their proper state of freedom and resist, unanimous in agreeing to blame you for their ruined day when they hear the door roll shut, you who seem to them to be in charge of everything, why not the weather as well?

At first, they might well knock and kick the hardwood walls, squeal in irritation at one another, raking teeth on the wire mesh between them. You begin work and the horses recognize their protests are getting them nowhere. The objections temper to a hum of frustrated energy, like the *zum* of membranous bee wings.

Stall by stall you muck and rake, spread fresh bedding, bang ice from the buckets and refill with fresh water. Gradually, they resign themselves. Only the wheelbarrow going in and out today. But room service is here. It must be nearly dinner time.

When the three slices of hay lands by their hooves and the evening's shot of grain pours into the corner feeder, their fretted hum mutes to the sweet melody of communal munching, a hymn they go on with long after the lights go dark and you have left.

At St. Joseph's we had a single classroom for each grade level and every classroom had a shelf or two under the windows known as "the library." I devoured what books that library had to offer. At St. Joseph's those offerings heavily favored the lives of the saints.

Hagiography is as stripped down as a comic book. Good versus evil. Condensed and potent. These tales were nothing like the politically corrected, Disneyfied versions of fairy tales children are exposed to nowadays. The stories I was consuming were as raw and violent as any Greek or Roman myth. No coincidence there, since the adherents of those very gods and goddesses were the contemporaries of many of these saints and the epic struggle of Christianity to supplant that system was what structured the stories.

Saints are classified by the major characteristic that had led to their canonization. As an elementary school girl ingesting the St. Joseph School library offerings, my favorite saint category was *virgin and martyr*. I was surely not privy to the biological specifics of what *virgin* meant. My understanding of the word, used as a kind of honorific for the female saints, was something along the lines of pure and, like our teachers the nuns, married to "the Blessed Bridegroom," Christ, and never to those earthly men who lusted for your beauty. At least three of our nuns, Sister Rose Sharon, Sister Ann Louise, and Sister Anne Bernadette, fourth, fifth, and sixth grade, respectively, were young and pretty, and in their wimples, veils, and long robes, dressed similarly to the illustrations of these long-ago saints, which no doubt contributed to my sense that those ancient stories could still be directly contemporaneous to me. My vague comprehension of what *lusted* meant ran along the lines of a loss of free will and options. A loss the virgin martyrs taught me was something to be strenuously resisted.

The martyr part there was never any obfuscation about — the gruesome death was always described in exacting detail as a measure of the glory attained. Joan of Arc — one of my favorites because she was French, as I was French; because she had escaped the limited female role she had been born to; and because she was reported to have been devoted to her horse — was tied to a stake and burned alive.

Only females were labeled *virgin and martyr*. A male would be simply *martyr*. St. Lawrence, they tied to a grill and roasted over slow coals to draw out the agony but Lawrence was so on fire for the Lord that he joked to his torturers, *Turn me over, I'm done on this side.* They obliged. Yes, this is what the nine-year-old was reading.

What did I learn from all of this? Children don't always take the lessons we think we are imparting. Children home in on the details that validate what they are most famished for. Perhaps that's what we all do with stories. Incorporate what we're famished for.

One whole school year my assigned seat was in the back corner of the classroom beside the three-foot-high statue of the Blessed Virgin Mary. I use that particular title of Mary's because the BVM statue is an iconic pose. Goggle *Blessed Virgin Mary statue* and even now you can see exactly what the one in my school room decades ago looked like. The statue in my classroom was on the shelf over the radiator so rather than her beatific face, or her arms stretched out to show both her obedience to the will of God and her reaching out to help we humans still here on earth, what I stared at all those months were her feet. Beneath her snow-white shift and gilt-edged, sky-blue cloak, Mary is balanced on the ball of the earth's globe, her bare feet crushing the serpent of the evil in this world. Here's a woman who could plant her unprotected feet on the squirming snake of the devil and never lose her alabaster calm. The lesson I took: don't mess with Mary. When it came to women, don't presume you know the interior from looking at the exterior.

Gil and Marion were married early in September of 1947. The Boston lumber firm she'd worked for hired two women to take her place and my mother threw her formidable energies into motherhood and housekeeping. By their third month as a married couple, she was pregnant. Gilbert Jr. was born just days after their first anniversary, and I arrived two years later. That Christmas Eve, they moved into their first house, the newly built colonial on Rose Hill Drive in Cranston, pulling a fresh-cut tree into the empty rooms along with the packing boxes. They put up and decorated the tree, then Mom, Dad, toddler, and infant arrived at Mémère and Pépère's for the family Christmas Eve party. Afterward Mom settled the children to sleep in their unfamiliar rooms and made up their own bed while Dad pulled Santa duties.

Two and a half years passed and there was another boy; two more years and another girl. At that stage Mom was still vacuuming the back of the refrigerator and ironing underwear and diapers. She was by nature a perfectionist but more than that she knew firsthand what a luxury it was to be home with the house and children, supported by your man. It was a luxury her own mother never had. My grandfather was a hard worker and steadily employed but at jobs that couldn't cover all the bills. Sometime in the early years of my grandparents' marriage, Gramps' young aunt Nan, who had been only twelve when my grandfather was born, came over from Ireland and moved in with them. Nan never married, never moved out. Nan and my Nana shared childcare and housework, along with work outside the home. When my mother quit her job to marry and keep house for a man, in her family that was a middle-class dream fulfilled.

❖

I did have some favorites among the saints who were not martyrs, happy to know there were pathways to eternal happiness that did not involve enduring torture. The one "doctor of the church" among my favorites was Augustine, who interested me mostly because of the connection I felt for having been born on his feast day. I was probably in high school before I learned that August the month was named for the emperor Augustus not the saint Augustine.

But mostly I was drawn to the women saints and it tended to be the contemplatives whose lives were devoted to thought, reading, and writing. The Rubens painting of Saint Teresa of Ávila shows her writing in a book with a quill. Saint Thérèse of Lisieux, the Little Flower, led a life of purity and devotion and died of tuberculosis at twenty-four, a life plan that, to a fourth grader, seemed doable. The Little Flower's fame was spread through the spiritual autobiography, letters, poems, and plays she left behind. Based on the role models offered — Sleeping Beauty, Snow White, Pocahontas, Cinderella, 1950s Barbie whose only interests and accoutrements were high fashion, a convertible, and her neutered boyfriend, Ken — given the narrow range of role models on offer, if a little girl wanted to grow up to be a freestanding intellectual whose worth was not attached to that of any man, sainthood looked like a promising model to aim for.

What kind of crap did my mother not take?

The crap she didn't take from any of us kids had many manifestations but at base it resolved to *do as I tell you*.

Did I set dinner in front of you? This was a rhetorical question. My mother was an excellent cook who had learned the art not from her own mother but from the immigrant Italian lady who lived in the apartment above them their first two years of marriage, and from her French-Canadian mother-in-law.

We think of the French in general as excellent cooks but my Mémère was a standout even in the company of her equally French family and community.

On my maternal side, my Nana's approach was more utilitarian, which may just have been a function of circumstances.

My Nana grew up the second oldest of seven on a small landholding in rural County Galway, an area of the Gaeltacht in western Ireland well-acquainted with privation. I have said "landholding," though I do not in fact know for sure who "held" that land legally during her childhood. What I do know is that the land and the ruins of the stone cottage she grew up in remain in the Keady family today.

Through her childhood, and through the early decade or so of her immigration, being grateful you had it to eat was a high enough expectation for food in my Nana's life. My mother's younger siblings remember better times than these but my mother was the firstborn of her family. She would have been seven when the Depression hit. What my mother told me she remembered from those days was boiled potatoes with egg cooked in with the potatoes to save on fuel. She remembers warming herself winter mornings down in the kitchen by the open oven door, and their early house by the dog biscuit factory where sometimes the factory owner would come out to the little porch and offer the children playing in the yard "a cookie." Which she would take if it was offered.

It is not hard to understand then that if my mother set perfectly good food down in front of you, she expected you to eat it. Even if it was lima beans. Even if it was blood pudding, a French-Canadian use-every-scrap concoction my father inexplicably had a taste for.

Other crap my mother didn't take from any of us kids:

> *I don't want to hear another word out of you.*
> *No child of mine will ever . . .*
> *I'll give you something to cry about.*
> *Are you cruisin' for a bruisin'?*
> *Because I said so.*

She was a woman in mastery of mothering, housewifery, a woman who could turn out a clean house, four spit-shined children lined up in descending order, and still have her own make-up perfectly applied, her outfit artfully coordinated and accessorized. As one of the kids, you had the lives of neighborhood kids and your cousins to compare your own life with and thus, though you might have private complaints about how it was all achieved, you knew you were witnessing competency of the highest order.

America has two origin stories that to this day we retell to every school child: John Smith and Pocahontas, and the First Thanksgiving. That first Thanksgiving brings us back to Mashpee, where Popponesset is located.

What we know of that first Thanksgiving we have through the accounts of two Mayflower survivors who were present at that event, Edward Winslow, and the group's governor, William Bradford. In his journal, which was later published as *On Plimoth Plantation*, Bradford wrote that after that first harvest of 1621 had been gathered: "Some . . . were exercised in fishing, about cod and bass and other fish, of which they took good store," as well as water fowl and many "wild turkeys." In a letter to a friend in England (later published in the promotional pamphlet that is now known as *Mort's Relation*), Winslow reported "our harvest being gotten in, our governor sent four men on fowling, that we might after a special manner rejoice together . . . at which time . . . many of the Indians coming amongst us, and amongst the rest their greatest king Massasoit, with some ninety men, whom for three days we entertained and feasted, and they went out and killed five Deer, which they brought to the Plantation and bestowed on our governor, and upon the Captain and others."

Because of Bradford's careful records, we know there were forty-eight Pilgrims and five servants at that first Thanksgiving — all the survivors who remained from the Mayflower. Plus, 100 Native Americans. Or, to upgrade our knowledge base, 100 Mashpee Wampanoag men, including their leader Massasoit. Twice as many native people as English, four grown women, five adolescent girls, and two young girls for a total of eleven females out of the nearly 150 people in attendance.

Even a schoolchild such as myself who had already spent considerable time in the actual town of Mashpee knew the Thanksgiving story only as Pilgrims and "Indians," and like any American child in Georgia, Montana, or wherever, my impression of the "Indians" came from the Little Golden books, grade-school textbooks, and classroom pageants where the indigenous peoples were represented in the image of the Saturday morning Western TV shows and B-reel movies we were all watching. How else would we have recognized them as Indians? This is America passing on its history to the new generation but the history being imparted is not the history of an event but the history of a narrative of national identity. An allegory of welcome, collaboration, humility, generosity, and gratitude.

During the inaugural term of the nation's institution of the presidency, George Washington called for one national day of Thanksgiving, but subsequent presidents did not turn that into an annual event specifically because they were concerned to preserve the founding principle of separation of church and state. The tradition of Thanksgiving as a constitutive event in our national history does not become enshrined as a national holiday until 1863, when Abraham Lincoln, in the wake of Gettysburg, reaches for a unifying metaphor to salve a sundered people.

Were we Catholic school children supposed to be learning orthodoxy and certainty? From the *Baltimore Catechism* I learned the allure of rhythm, assonance, anaphora and epiphora, antiphony: *Why did God make us?* God made us to show forth His goodness and to share with us His everlasting happiness in heaven. *What must we do to gain the happiness of heaven?* To gain the happiness of heaven we must know, love, and serve God in this world.

Along with the pleasures of rhetorical magic was the pull of narrative. Presented with a story such as omnipotent God so loved the world that He gave us His only begotten Son, knowing we humans were going to murder him in the most horrific way we could come up with — you know, so we could share in that everlasting happiness — what I concluded was that life is deeply and fundamentally mysterious, awesome in the fullest sense. I learned the concept of Keats's Negative Capability: when a man (or a little girl) is capable of being in uncertainties, mysteries, doubts, without any irritable reaching after fact and reason.

Here in February, we wake to a world furred with snow. The trees have turned to lungs, every bronchus, bronchiole, and alveoli of their boughs and branches limned with powder, snow so soft that each least puff of wind exhales in a cloud, an immanence like the apparition of our own core in the cold, when our every exhalation clouds around us, an evaporating halo.

In her interactions with other grownups, my mother was polished, professional when the situation called for it, and friendly when warranted but she didn't back down from the way mechanics or car salesmen treated women in the 1950s and '60s, or from a pediatrician (always male, the nurses were female) who might not be taking her child's condition with the seriousness it warranted. She was someone to be reckoned with. Someone no one rolled over.

But what was the crap she doled out to herself?

> *I am not an alcoholic.*
> *I am not an alcoholic.*

Which prompts me to say to you, Dear Reader, don't give up on us yet.

A line like *she was an alcoholic* is a finish line, an *I don't need to hear any more* line. A line I avoid saying because I know how adept that line is in erecting a prefab narrative, a ready-made story that eclipses all subsequent stories.

And the dead can't defend themselves.

No one I say that line to now can ever meet my mother, can ever be influenced by contact with her to see her in a broader context than the wall of that alcoholic storyline that has just sprung up between her and anything further you're likely to hear. So how can I say that line when it shouts down every other thing I say about her?

I have the good fortune to have several friends I have been close to for decades. When I met one of these friends, we were college students, the age when one is typically still in the process of leaving behind the domicile of one's parents' marriage. The father she had then was fiercely bright and competent, but so meticulously demanding that his prodding and attempts at control had caused the firstborn of the family to rebel by sabotaging his own considerable prospects as a way to pull his life out of the father's orbit, a spinout my friend's brother could be said to have never fully righted from. This father was a master of the silent-treatment punishment and control in his dealings with his wife.

But this father had the gift of time. He became over time a doting grandfather who knew when it wasn't his place to interfere, and then an adamantly devoted caretaker to that wife as her memory gradually drifted from her.

My mother has neither the chance to defend herself, nor the luxury of all those decades to grow into herself.

What I hope for is to be able to say *she was an alcoholic* and still have the option to say other true things about her.

Other words/narratives that block the ears: in Ireland the fault line of religion, which is really a fault line of politics, of colonization and victimization. In America, race. Which again is a fault line of politics, of colonization and victimization.

In light of the tyrannical history of created categories such as these, is there any necessity to delineating what is dangerous about the human imagination?

Late in February in Mediterranean Rome, snow limns the vaulted arches of the Colosseum, frosting the surfaces like a gargantuan wedding cake. Meanwhile in the Arctic, four months deep into the murk of polar night, temperatures rise above the melting point, the ice sheet softening in the dark.

If one believes these anomalies to be not anomalies but results, what does one do with that belief?

March

The hem of our third nor'easter in a two-week span brushes us as March begins, the cold of those storms sweeping in on the heels of a February thaw that had coaxed the tulips inches above their bed and lured the songbirds north. The leathery little wet-suits of the tulip leaves go limp and then sink beneath the March snow.

In North Carolina the swamps are freezing again, the alligators poking their snouts above the water's surface just as liquid congeals to solid, icing them in.

Days pass and the frozen reptiles thaw out and swim away. It's called *brumation*, a state analogous to hibernation, a talent apparently atavistically stored away in the alligator DNA. For climate deniers, such stories embolden their cavalier presumptions that we needn't worry as we'll "think of something."

The mother I remember from my childhood was formidable: strong-willed, able and dependable, tender and terrifying, talented, demanding, sensitive, productive, passionate, unpredictable, admirable, and, yes, at times pathetic. By the time I was nine or ten I knew what she was unable to let herself know: she was an alcoholic.

Your basic skid-row alcoholic is a trauma victim, torn and bleeding, the damage obvious to all. A high-functioning alcoholic like my mother is more like early-stage cancer, a calamity inside while the outside surface holds together, can even have the appearance of health, an insidious ruse that keeps one in denial and persistently away from help. Particularly in the 1950s and '60s, when alcoholism was considered a moral failing, not a medical condition. And for a woman? a lady? How hard she'd worked to be a lady.

The drinking began as purely social. What I think I know about what happened and why, in all likelihood would be only pieces of the truth but those are the pieces I have. I remember "The Bridge Club," a rotating ritual of weekend card games that were probably relaxation to the men. For the women they were occasions that put your housekeeping prowess, your mothering skills, your cooking expertise, and your own personal charms all up for evaluation at once.

It takes significant energy and will to make a three-bedroom house that houses six people, including four young children, look as if it's fully furnished but no one actually lives there. My mother was the hands-on, micromanaging general and we four children were her forces. "It's a remarkable thing about skin: you can go ahead and get your hands dirty because God has made hands endlessly washable. They aren't going to wear out," she told me when I balked at hand-scrubbing the toilet bowl with the attention to detail she demanded.

When every dust mote had been routed, every sill between window and screen wiped, every inch of carpet vacuumed, and every floor scoured corner-to-corner, food preparation began. How we loved that part! The icebox cake with its layers of dark chocolate cookie wafers and clouds of whipped cream. When the cake was complete, one got the bowl, one the spoon, and a mixer beater for each of the other two. Dinner those nights was simple and early. Baths and shampoos all around and into our Carter pajamas. Always Carter pajamas since Nana made them in the factory she could walk to across the square from her house. Pajamas and underwear for Christmas from Nana and Gramps were immutables. While Mom bathed the kids, Dad set up the card tables and folding chairs in the immaculate living room.

Then Mom and Dad dressed while we sidled about the house, avoiding denting the sofa cushions or mussing the *Ladies' Home Journals* arranged on the coffee table. When the guests arrived, we children were expected to appear briefly, answer questions respectfully, and on cue head off to bed. If Mom caught us sneaking a cashew out of one of the pretty glass bowls of mixed nuts, or reaching for one of the broken rounds in the fluffy pile of potato chips, she'd tell us pointedly, "FHB." Family Hold Back. It meant get your mitts out of the chips; there's time enough tomorrow for you to have some if there're any left over.

Liquor was always a feature of those bridge parties. The chime of ice in glasses mixes with the melody of soft voices as we lay upstairs waiting for sleep. Liquor had had very little place in my mother's life before she met my father, but liquor was an assumed part of her new social life. At first mixed drinks were just another recipe to be learned.

A social drinker himself, with no experience with alcoholism, in a culture that still associated the condition with weak will, moral depravity, and winos in the gutter, it could not have been easy for either of my parents to recognize the earliest signs but in retrospect my father settled on Penny McCarthy.

The McCarthys moved in across the street before I'd even started school. So far as I know, the initial attraction was proximity and Katie McCarthy, a golden-haired little girl exactly my age, a playmate for Christine. Soon the mothers were sharing coffee and conversation in our kitchen, while Katie joined in impromptu games of Mother may I? and furious pedaling of tricycles around the grassy-middled, dual-track cement driveway. It was Penny McCarthy, my father maintained, who introduced my mother to daytime drinking.

When did morning coffee give way to morning Manhattans, and why? Those aren't questions the child can answer. Mrs. McCarthy, we children understood, was suspect from the start — the beauty-parlored hair, the clothes, the one and only child. The vague sense of moral lassitude that clung to Mrs. McCarthy was confirmed when the McCarthys divorced, a shocking failure women found it hard to hold their heads up after in the mid-1950s. But hold her head up she did. Penny McCarthy moved herself and her daughter back into her mother's house.

❖

We live by story, narratives that give shape and meaning to our lives as individuals, and to the larger context of our individual lives, stories we label "history" and "national identity." In addition to the stories told, are the stories untold. Untold stories may be suppressed by the principals, or prevented from being told by the powerful who prefer a different story. Can a buried story resurrected have an impact?

Despite the Pilgrims' description of having landed amidst a howling wilderness, they actually sited the settlement they named Plymouth atop the abandoned indigenous village of Patuxet, with the natives' cleared fields to get them started. Patuxet was available to the English settlers because in the years just before the Mayflower nosed into Cape Cod Bay, an epidemic of some one of the European diseases for which the native populations had no immunity had wiped out the Wampanoag village — part of a widespread plague during 1616 to 1619 that the Wampanoags and other indigenous groups along the coast from Maine to Cape Cod call The Great Dying, and which William Bradford referred to in *On Plimouth Plantation* as "the good hand of God," which "favored our beginnings" by "sweeping away great multitudes of the natives . . . that he might make room for us."

One of the few, if not the only, survivor of the village of Patuxet escaped The Great Dying because he was in London when the epidemic hit. According to Paula Peters, who I'm about to introduce you to, this information is common knowledge among the Wampanoags and is also well-documented in the diaries of English mariners, but you might not have been exposed to these details in school, so let me sketch in a bit more of this backstory to provide context to the part you do know.

As always, when we enter the past, we enter wanting the truth. What we understand as the truth. As always, when we enter the past, what we have are the stories, and the tellers. And what we piece together out of language into the shape that represents our individual and idiosyncratic understanding of *truth*.

Here is how Paula Peters of the contemporary Wampanoag tells the story. Paula Peters's bona fides as a scholar of Wampanoag history include that she once served as director of Marketing and Public Relations for the Wampanoag Indian Program at the historical reenactment site Plimoth Plantation, and she represented Wampanoag interests on the Board of Directors for Plymouth, 400 Inc., the nonprofit dedicated to commemorating the 400th anniversary of the Mayflower's 1620 landing (a commemoration that actually ended up considerably muted by the pandemic of our day, COVID-19). Peters is currently associated with Harvard University's Peabody Museum of Archaeology and Ethnology, on whose website she is described as "an independent scholar and writer of Native, and particularly Wampanoag history."

Six years before the Mayflower, in 1614, there had been a two-ship exploratory expedition from England, charged with mapping the coasts of Maine and Massachusetts. The captain in charge of the expedition was John Smith — yes, the same John Smith we associate with Virginia and the Pocahontas narrative of nation-building, in which culture contact is a love story of masculine European enterprise and feminine American availability and welcome. We can come back to Pocahontas, but right now we're with John Smith in New England 1614, not Virginia 1608.

The fact that even today we refer to that region of the United States as "New England" is credited to Smith on that 1614 voyage, and as Paula Peters tells it, what Smith had learned in Virginia about negotiation versus his initial impulse — confrontation and brute force — when dealing with indigenous peoples serves him well in his subsequent, more diplomatic encounters with the coastal natives in Maine and Massachusetts.

Smith's subordinate, Thomas Hunt, captain of the secondary ship, seems to have been unconvinced by Smith's long-range planning and politic approach to dealing with the indigenous population, however, and when Smith returned to England with a cargo full of furs and fish, leaving Hunt to supposedly finish similarly loading his ship with fish, Hunt traded on the goodwill Smith had built up to lure aboard twenty Wampanoag men from the village of Patuxet, and later seven more from Nauset, with a false promise of trade. In fact, Hunt kidnapped the men with the plan of taking the captives to Malaga, Spain, to be sold into slavery. Unsurprisingly, Hunt's perfidy deeply soured relations between the Wampanoags and the English.

Of those twenty-seven captives from Patuxet and Nauset, only the Patuxet man named Tisquantum ever surfaces again in the oral or written historical records of either group. One version of the story says, hey, we don't know how he ended up in London; another version (the story Paula Peters recounts) says some of those captive American natives were saved by Spanish monks who stalked the slave market for the purpose of rescuing as many as they could, that Tisquantum was one of those saved by the friars and that eventually he made it to London, where he learned to speak English and was exposed to English customs. Torn from family, village, landscape, even the homeland that is one's mother tongue, Tisquantum spends five years working out a way back home to Patuxet. He eventually manages to convince the New England Company investors that his language skills and cultural knowledge will make him the perfect go-between to try to repair the damaged trading relations between England and the native groups in coastal Massachusetts, if only they'll get him back home.

Imagine Tisquantum's despair in 1619, to finally reach Patuxet only to find everyone in his village dead. Everyone.

Tisquantum is taken in by the remains of the neighboring Wampanoag group, the Mashpees, across the Cape on Vineyard Sound. Taken in, but bilingual border crosser that he now is, not necessarily wholly trusted.

Perhaps you've already figured out that Tisquantum is the man the Pilgrims called Squanto (according to Paula Peters a name he was commonly known by, rather than an early example of Anglo-Americans taking it upon themselves to anglicize non-English names into syllables they were comfortable with). The Wampanoags' major concern in 1620 when the Mayflower sailed into Cape Cod Bay was the threat that, in their decimated state, their group would be overrun by their traditional enemies to the west, the Narragansetts. When this ragged band of Englishmen shows up, the Wampanoags want to evaluate whether or not the English might make useful allies for them to help strengthen their position vis-à-vis the Narragansetts, so they send Tisquantum to go live among the Pilgrims and act as something between an ambassador and a spy.

The rest of this story you know. By the time the Wampanoags realized the English were a greater threat to them than the Narragansetts and the various Native groups tried to band together in what's known as King Philip's War — King Philip being what the English called the Mashpee Wampanoag leader Metacom, who led the Native American resistance in 1675 to 1676 — it was already too late to oust the Europeans. King Philip's War wiped out 40 percent of what Wampanoags there were and at the end of the war, most of the male survivors were sold into slavery in the West Indies. Many of what women and children survived were enslaved in New England.

But there were survivors who remained on the land their ancestors had always lived on, particularly centered in Mashpee and at Aquinnah out on Martha's Vineyard. These groups continued as many aspects of their culture as they could.

For my eighth birthday, my mother bought me three horseback riding lessons from the riding academy at Goddard Park in Warwick, and a complete outfit of equestrian clothes she went to an actual tack shop to purchase. Because how could I have my three lessons without proper attire?

Can you understand how deeply thrilled I was by the gift if I tell you that more than sixty years on, I can clearly recall standing before the mirror in the front bedroom I now shared with my sister Janine, bathing in the glorious sight of me in riding clothes? The exotic, gleaming-new clothes validated a me I aspired to be with all my heart. I remember every detail. The shirt was white with pinstripes of metallic gold, the collar neatly closed off with a matching gold string tie, and then jodhpurs in a coordinating creamy buff color.

I understand now that my mother had outfitted me for Western riding on the top half and English riding on the bottom, but I was blissfully unaware of those details at the time. I mean every modicum of the word *blissful*.

The horse they put me on for my lessons was named Sherrie, a palomino whose golden coat complemented my golden outfit. Radiance. In three lessons, we progressed as far as walk, and a bit of trot.

For the next five years, each August my father would take me to Goddard Park for my one-hour birthday ride on those leafy trails along Narragansett Bay. One hour a year. A ritual of desire to be among beasts I paradoxically both longed to be with and feared. Their majesty, and their muscular power — like some kind of metaphor for potential and capacity — intoxicating and unnerving. The embodiment of mystery: how could I be so drawn to this being so unlike myself? Horses elicited for me the full spectrum of *thrilling* from delight to fear.

All of us buy into and shape our lives around some amount of crap, some dangerous fiction we cling to with deadly determination. It can be dangerous fictions at the microlevel of our personal lives, such as when my mother would insist to herself that she was not an alcoholic, but often even more insidious are the community narratives we swallow collectively, stories that have fit the expectations and ambitions of whole groups of us so perfectly as to make us believe the narratives are not invented accounts but something we understand as the actual nature of the world.

Four-hundred-year-old blind spots are easier to discern than the beam in our own eye, so we're going to pop back to John Smith and the Puritans, respectively, to take a look at some powerful stories that shaped world events, despite what to us, all these years later, is the obvious self-serving nature of those stories.

When you discover a two-continent-sized landmass you had not previously known existed, this news takes some explaining. When Christopher Columbus and other European adventurers set off to explore the possibility of reaching what they referred to as the Orient by traveling West, what they had in mind was trading with the civilizations — China, India, Japan — that they knew to be there. When instead they found North and South America, their sense of what they had thought of as the known world imploded, in a transition that was both instantaneous and drawn out. The persistence even today of Columbus's misnomer "Indians," for instance, is a familiar marker of the tenacity of old beliefs even in the face of stubborn new evidence.

In the untidy scramble to redefine the "New World" all sides were finding themselves in, one might expect one possible narrative the Europeans could have settled on would be, oh look, civilizations we hadn't known about, let's trade with them instead of, or in addition to, the Chinese, Indians, Japanese. In fact, that approach did appear but it was not the storyline that dominated.

❖

European literature of the day is one good way to get some insight into how the elite were thinking about these worldview-shattering new discoveries. The inventing and recalibrating went on for a long time; some interesting milestones along the way would be Thomas More's *Utopia* (1516); Shakespeare's *The Tempest* (1610); Francis Bacon's *New Atlantis* (1626); and Jonathan Swift's *Island of the Houyhnhnms* (1726). Notice how long humans went on working and reworking their understanding of the meaning(s) of their "new world."

For our purposes, a few lines from John Donne's poem, "To His Mistress Going to Bed," will give us insight into one recurring European assumption about these "new" lands. Donne's life spanned from 1572 until 1631, so the poem would be roughly contemporaneous to *The Tempest*. Recommending *Full nakedness!* for the mistress in the poem's title, Donne entreats her

> Licence my roving hands, and let them go,
> Before, behind, between, above, below.
> O my America! my new-found-land.

Still a sexy poem after all these years and yet, what does it mean to think of the Americas as a mistress in need of merely a few blandishments in order for her to offer her sweet favors to you freely? Circa 1575, the Flemish artist Theodor Galle did an engraving of a drawing by Jan van der Straet, that gives us a graphic of this same understanding of "America." Galle's image is easy enough to find online, because his engraving is part of the permanent collection of the National Gallery in Washington, DC, in keeping with the image's important role in our nation's sense of identity.

If you're thinking poem-*schmoem*, what does poetry have to do with real life? I could argue about the different role poetry played in the seventeenth-century as opposed to the twenty-first, or point out that John Donne was a significant public figure in his day who served in Parliament for more than a decade, but instead let's just shift to a variation on this theme that you will instantly recognize as still being an indispensable parable we as a nation use even now to introduce juvenile Americans to a sense of what that culture clash meant and how it gave rise to our present nation. Right up to the present day, the story of the first

Thanksgiving and the story of Pocahontas and John Smith are the two narratives we persist in using to establish the moral legitimacy of our national origins.

❖

Only one eyewitness to the event left behind a written record of the iconic encounter of the English with the Powhatans of what we now call Virginia, but for centuries official American culture gave every indication of being comfortable with the fact that we had the story only from the male/European point of view. Surely there have to have been those all along who recognized what was crap about that approach.

John Smith actually wrote about his adventure three times — three distinctly different versions of the one event from the same author/eyewitness, only one of which we have enshrined in national lore as the meaning of the encounter. That's a good clue that there are two kinds of truth going on here: there's the *what happened, facts on the ground* kind of truth, and there's the *what did we accept and act upon as the meaning of what happened* kind of truth.

Each time Smith recounts this story, his aim is to promote colonization and to promote himself as a premier colonizer. I'm quoting Smith here from a source that preserves the seventeenth-century spelling and usages of the original rather than a source that has transcribed the original into modern English (the same is true for the quotes from John Winthrop in the December section). I trust the parts quoted will not be difficult for you to decipher. The "first draft," as it were, of the story that would become national mythology, was written in Smith's journal soon after the actual encounter and published in London that same year, 1608, as a pamphlet under the title "A True Relation of such Occurrences and Accidents of Noate as Has Hapned in Virginia since the First Planting of that Collony..."

Version 1 is the *here's-somebody-new-to-trade-with* rendition. Smith admits to his feelings of admiration upon first meeting their "Emperour" proudly lying on a raised platform, covered with raccoon skins and "richly hung with manie Chaynes of great Pearles about his neck." Powhatan "kindly welcomed me with good wordes, and great Platters of sundrie Victuals, assuring me his friendship, and my libertie within foure days," Smith tells us, concluding with "and thus, having with all the kindness hee could devise, sought to content me, hee sent me home, with 4. men: one that usually carried my Gowne and Knapsacke after me, two other loded with bread, and one to accompanie me," a description which may surprise you to hear, given the version we've all been raised on. The first time Smith tells the story, no brain-beating is threatened and no one named Pocahontas even shows up.

When you consider the mythology we've grown up on — the story of love-at-first-sight between America (Pocahontas) and her handsome young Europe (John Smith), leading to the happily-ever-after we know of as the United States

— it's also disorienting to realize that John Smith the actual person left Virginia in 1610 (gravely injured in a gunpowder accident, he went back to England to recuperate) and never managed to make it back to Virginia.

As part of his unsuccessful efforts to get back there, though, he had occasion twice more to rewrite and revise his initial account of the encounter and turn it into something his potential sponsors could find more palatable than that original, "Hey, we discovered interesting new people to trade with" narrative that implicitly implied the "new" land was already spoken for. The adroit John Smith realized spin control was called for. A 1616 letter to the devout Queen Anne with its virginal, child Pocahontas whom God himself has converted is the middle version, but in 1624, Smith publishes his best-known work, *The Generall Historie of Virginia, New-England, and the Summer Isles*, and it is here that we find the story that gave rise to the mythology that makes John Smith and Pocahontas household names even today.

Between what you want to do and what you believe you ought to do, the moral low road and the moral high road, there is often a distinct gap. Think of the refinements we make in our own busy minds to the account of some misadventure we've just had as we drive home and picture telling what has happened to family and friends — the creativity that goes into shading the description of just what our actions and intentions were in what transpired. The story the Puritans told themselves, and that non-Puritans were quick to see the utility of, was that the Americas were a "New Eden." "[T]he good hand of God" swept "away great multitudes of the natives . . . that he might make room for us." How could one hope for a higher moral purpose than fulfilling God's plan?

In the telling and retelling Europeans went through in coming to terms with the meaning of their enterprise there in North America, the hard truth is that for both the 1607 settlers in Jamestown and the 1620 settlers in Plymouth, they would never have survived their first winter without the help of the native groups where they had landed. How to make sense of that information when your preferred understanding of the world was that the indigenous peoples of this "new" land were readily replaceable because they were irremediably inferior to Europeans? The human imagination is up to such a task.

In Smith's 1624 account of his initial encounter with the Powhatans, the matter-of-fact descriptions of the 1608 version (*on each side sitting on mats were ranged his chief men*) morphs to the melodrama of *200 grim Courtiers staring at him as if he were a monster*; while, *he welcomed me with kind words and great platters of sundry victual, assuring me of his friendship and my freedom* becomes instead *having feasted him after their best barbarous manner they could, a long consultation was held, but the conclusion was, two great stones were brought before Powhatan: then as many as could layd hands on him, dragged him to them, and thereon laid his head, and being ready with their clubs, to beate out his braines,*

Pocahontas the Kings dearest daughter, when no intreaty could prevaile, got his head in her armes, and laid her owne vpon his to saue him from death.

There's the story we still tell American children today to explain to them the meaning of our national origin. This 1624 version embodies a truth about European desires and ambitions that, while it likely differs from the facts, embodies presumptions that had a more profound impact than the facts themselves were able to exert.

Our contemporary sense of the story now is occluded by the 1995 Disney Princess version with its suddenly egalitarian marriage model between technologically savvy John Smith and eco-sensitive Pocahontas, but consider for a moment what the power dynamics between the genders were in 1624. Or 1724. Or 1824. Or 1924. For close to 400 years that origin story was telling us clearly who was in charge, who was submissive, who got to speak, who should remain silent, whose opinion mattered, who could be discounted, who should know her place.

In Jamestown the narrative is that the "good" natives like Pocahontas instinctively recognize European superiority, as a good woman "naturally" recognizes the superiority of her man (as God intended: see Bible). In Plymouth the origin story is that they are God's Pilgrims, tasked by the Almighty with shaping a shining city on the hill.

The birds on Galapagos had no fear of humans but the black-necked swans were birds of passage — they had been elsewhere and could not be caught by humans because they brought knowledge with them from elsewhere and knew to be afraid.

Like many a future writer of my age, I devoured Nancy Drew novels. What a balm it was to read the world back into resolution with every book. Those books were so reliably formulaic, I learned my first lessons in narrative structure from them. And that fusty vocabulary. I liked that with a certain regularity there would be a word I'd never before encountered and I would have to look the word up in the dictionary, but that day I poked a finger between the pages to hold my place and went to ask Dad the unfamiliar word. I meant the question as a little olive branch to offer, a way to steer the conversation at least temporarily away from the conflagration of our family.

"Fugitive?" he said. "That's what you and your mother were last night."

Last night is why I was home in the middle of the day reading Nancy Drew, why I wasn't at school with my brothers and sister.

The terms of the argument are forgotten — likely to the child the terms of the argument had always been inexplicable. I remember the shouting, the suitcase my mother packed and my father wrenching it from her hand, the clothes spilling out onto the floor. My mother called the police from upstairs, called me upstairs to choose a few of my own things to pack.

I remember watching from the top of the stairs as my father opened the front door. How the two policemen filled the doorframe. How dark and broad and menacing, how they carried their darkness and their guns into our living room.

Did she want him arrested? No, she wanted to pack a few things, to take her oldest daughter and leave for the night.

The cops stayed downstairs with my father and my siblings while we threw pajamas, underwear, a few things into the aluminum suitcase.

I'm sure we didn't go far. Alone in the car while my mother went in to register, I watched the neon sign: M-O-T-E-L. *This is my first time staying in a motel*, I thought to myself. The sign illuminated the branch of a tree, the trunk itself swallowed back into the darkness, and on the branch an owl, which I identified by its hooting. It sounded so much like the toys that teach the sounds of the animals as to be unmistakable.

I held the sighting of the owl close to my heart like a secret that would not hurt me.

Remember when you were a schoolchild and you thought history meant *the story of what happened?* John Smith is a good example of how even with only one reporter, there are often competing commentaries. In our sharply divided nation, the news and social media bring us multiple examples daily of the struggle to define one's own group, the other guy, and a national vision. The narrative of the inherent superiority of one group over other groups at the heart of the John Smith/Pocahontas story, still gospel to so many, continues to exert its insidious poison, often through the manipulations of powerful agents who actually see through the fallacies of the narrative while exploiting its power for their own purposes, just as the Puritan mythology of being on God's mission justified genocide and exploitation on a horrific scale. One small but historically iconic example: the land-grab doctrine of "Manifest Destiny" being sanitized by the

1872 painting *American Progress* by John Gast. Google will bring the image up for you easily if you are not already aware of it.

Powerful high-minded narratives constructed to justify (and obscure) mean-spirited and criminal actions are a consistent feature of humans in their private lives from the age at which one can first begin storytelling and in our collective lives throughout history. We can storytell ourselves into disbelieving the worst about ourselves, even when those stories can lead to our own destruction. The child of an alcoholic, an addict, a depressive, has witnessed this at the individual level. At a collective level, history and political science are a repository of witnessing the power and destructiveness of self-serving falsehoods over and over again. Good will prevail, we tell ourselves, and hope that's true despite all evidence to the contrary. But what if we run out of time? Nature will be nature. Some find solace in the narrative of a created world in which our species is the favorite son. It's a comforting story in the face of final questions for those who can believe.

As you might expect, at St. Joseph's School we wore uniforms — navy-blue jumpers with a pleated skirt and an SJS emblem over our hearts, a white blouse with Peter Pan collar, and a navy-blue bow tie — pretied with the two loops and exposed ends like the bow on a shoe. The only variation I was ever aware of that brought no murmur from the nuns about being out of uniform was March 17, St. Patrick's Day, when my mother would substitute a green bow for the navy, patting it in place while telling us we were, "wearing green for Gramps."

My mother's father had grown up in Tyrone, one of Ireland's northern counties. The political implications of Irish history were never discussed with us but we intuited from the start that "wearing of the green" was serious business. I was fifty and just returned from having visited both Derroe in Galway where my grandmother had grown up and Gramps' hometown of Aughnacloy before I learned that unlike his wife Nora who had immigrated for economic reasons, James Patrick had been put aboard a ship with his Uncle Jimmy by his own family who had decided it was the most prudent option before British authorities figured out it had been Jimmy Coyle who had pulled down the Union Jack in Aughnacloy and raised instead the flag of Ireland. My grandfather never saw Ireland or his family again.

Gramps maintained a flagpole at both the half-of-a-duplex house in Needham Heights, and the cottage at Popponesset, and all of us grandchildren learned from him the ceremonies of flag raising in the morning and lowering at dusk, and the intricacies of precisely folding the banner in the prescribed manner. A ritual of home, belonging, and respect for the privilege of having a home to belong to.

On the snow-shawled slope the house sits plump with satisfaction, the yellow-hearted stove pulses intently in the cellar, the bedrooms each sweetly podded with the proper sleepers, even the dogs curled and accounted for in soft circles on the floor while without the wind whistles its sharp tune beneath the brittle, patient stars.

April

In the garden, I'm clearing out the malodorous hulks of last season's final providers: December's kale and Brussels sprouts, reduced now to wrinkled trunks, the wadded mats of their leaves, and the unmistakable cruciferous smell. Beneath the kale skeletons in the raised bed, I find the winter Golgotha left behind by burrowing mammals, a long swath of cycloptic skulls: hollowed-out acorn shells. The chipmunks have wintered well.

Meanwhile, whose heart does not leap for the hallelujah of forsythia?

Writer Kerri Arsenault grew up in Mexico, Maine, an inland town in the Maine woods at the point where the Swift River empties into the much larger Androscoggin. Mexico was built by, and despoiled by, the papermaking mill across the Androscoggin in Rumford. Arsenault's 2020 investigative memoir *Mill Town: Reckoning with What Remains* is simultaneously an evocation of place, family, and home; a thoroughly researched chronicle of the environmental and health costs of industry — both papermaking and the Nestle Corporation's "mining" from the town's aquifer to market under Nestle's Poland Spring Water label; and a thoughtful consideration of economics, class, culture, and ethics, all through the lens of the town that provided her happy childhood, the livelihoods of her father and grandfather, and that seems to have brought so many of her loved ones to an early death. What the book has to say about pollution, economics, and the health of the planet applies to us all, but one of the book's draws for me was that Arsenault and I share a Franco-American connection. The Arsenault family is of Acadian descent while the Gelineaus are Quebecois, but the documentation that Arsenault's book provides about the French-Canadian immigrant experience in New England applies to Acadians and Quebecois alike and has a direct bearing on my paternal ancestors' lives.

According to careful genealogical research done by members of my extended clan, who I do not personally know, but who my father and uncles had confidence in, the Gelineau family line began on this continent in 1730, when the recently widowed Étienne Gélineau immigrated to Montreal in New France, along with his son François. We have family members in Montreal to this day but my great-grandfather Felix Gélineau, born 100 years before me in 1850, was the last of the generations that lead to me to have been born in Canada.

My Pépère, which is to say, my grandfather, Homer Arnold Gélineau, was born in 1887 in Haverhill, Massachusetts, the eighth child (of ten — not all of whom survived) of Felix and his wife Marie. Haverhill, Massachusetts is a textile mill town and one of the places French Canadian migrants flocked to in the second half of the nineteenth century.

In order to give a sense of the reception these French-speaking immigrants tended to receive, Kerri Arsenault quotes from an 1881 report of labor statistics from Massachusetts (just six years before my grandfather was born there). The report baldly stated,

> with some exceptions the Canadian French are the Chinese of the Eastern States. They care nothing for our institutions, civil, political, or educational. They do not come to make a home among us, to dwell with us as citizens and so become a part of us. They are horrid industrial invaders, not a stream of stable settlers. These people have one good trait. They're indefatigable workers, and docile. All they ask is to be set to work and they care little who rules them or how they are ruled, to earn all they can by no matter how many hours of toil, to live in the most beggarly way. To work them to the uttermost is about the only good use they can be put to.

That's the wording in an official government document. "The Chinese of the Eastern States" is one way of putting it, though I have more often heard the phrase "the *n*-word of New England." People "from away" often remark on how "white" Maine (and New England in general) is, but that misunderstands the history. "White" is an invented category that originally indicated specifically white Anglo-Saxon Protestant, what even in my childhood those of us excluded from that category tended to refer to as WASP. French Canadians, Irish, Jews, and various other non–Anglo Saxons were a thing apart from "Yankee." Arsenault quotes Waldo Pettingill, the first president of the paper mill there in her town in Maine, writing in 1907 in an editorial published in the *Rumford Falls Times*: "The entrance into our political, social, and industrial life of such vast masses of peasantry degraded below our utmost conceptions is a matter which no intelligent patriot can look upon without the gravest apprehension. They are beaten men from beaten races, representatives of the worst failure in the struggle for existence." What degraded the French in the eyes of their Yankee neighbors was that they did not promptly assimilate but rather continued to speak French among themselves, and continued to practice Catholicism. Many associate the Ku Klux Klan only with the South, but in fact the group was very active in many areas of the North, not least in New England, particularly in opposition to the French Canadians. Mark Paul Richard, professor of history and Canadian studies at the State University of New York at Plattsburgh, presents a sobering study of this dark history in his 2015 book, *Not a Catholic Nation: The Ku Klux Klan Confronts New England in the 1920s* (University of Massachusetts Press), which provides contextualizing history of the economic and social pressures of the times and the culture in which my grandparents were establishing themselves and raising their young family. In Arsenault's succinct words, "the KKK considered French Catholics subservient, a dark-skinned race that stole jobs, defiled American culture, and spoke in pagan tongues, Latin masses, French."

I don't have a complete timeline of my branch of the Gelineaus in the United States. The 1910 census report shows my great-grandparents Felix and Marie living in rented quarters in Providence, Rhode Island (my own birthplace), with their twenty-two-year-old son, Homer, and their nineteen-year-old daughter Annette. The census enumerates that all four family members speak English (that they were bilingual was not among the census questions) and are able to read and write.

The current Rhode Island State Capitol Building was built between 1895 and 1904. The imposing building was constructed in a style reminiscent of the US Capitol Building, out of Georgia marble and boasts one of the largest self-supported marble domes in the world. When during my childhood we would pass the State Capitol, my father would not infrequently remark that his grandfather was one of the men who built that dome and indeed, on the 1910 Census Felix Gelineau is listed as a self-employed marble worker. Interestingly for the times, nineteen-year-old Annette is identified as a bookkeeper who worked in an office while my twenty-two-year-old grandfather's occupation was listed as "salesman." Selling what I don't know. Pépère's draft card from 1918 indicates that eight years after the census, he was then the proprietor of his own restaurant, a story I never heard, but there is no question about Homer being entrepreneurial. Wrongheaded as they were about the dark, defeated, French-speaking peasantry, the "apprehensive patriots" were right about the hard-working part — indefatigable and optimistic described my Pépère, qualities my father surely inherited.

I don't have the details of how he met and married Valeda Robert between that 1910 census and his 1918 draft card that shows him to be married and the sole provider for his mother, his wife, and a child, which would have been my Uncle Bob, born in 1917. My Dad was born in 1919, so my grandmother had a toddler and was pregnant with her second during the 1918 flu pandemic.

I also don't have a detailed account of how Pépère made his fortune, but the general outline is that Homer had gone out to Goodyear Tire in Akron, Ohio, to learn the process of vulcanizing tires, then a new process and I believe not previously available in Rhode Island, or at least not widely available. At that time, my grandmother's brothers worked in the tire industry in Ohio; whether he met Valeda when he followed up on vulcanizing, or followed up on vulcanizing because he had met Valeda, I'm not clear on. What I do know is that he made a success of it. He had a bicycle shop that grew into my grandfather establishing himself as the first Chevrolet automobile dealer in the state of Rhode

Island. Gil Motors was on Washington Street, the main street of the then largely French-speaking Arctic section of West Warwick.

To accommodate their growing family, my grandparents bought the house farther down Washington Street, where the street turned residential rather than commercial. And soon they bought the beach house on Bay Ridge, and the elegant sailboat. In sharp contrast to my mother's memories, memories from my father's childhood and teenage years include the adrenaline rush of driving the shiny newly delivered Chevrolets off of the precipitous ramps of the transport trucks, and learning to sail the *Buccaneer* in Narragansett Bay.

I remember my mother and I visiting Penny McCarthy and my little friend Katie where they had moved to Penny's mother's house once or twice after my mother got her car.

How proud my mother was of that car. A 1957 Ford Fairlane 500, black with a glittering gold stripe on the side that flared as it reached the tail fins. Brand new so everything was exactly as she'd wanted it. MG 314. Vanity plates with her own initials, in a Gelineau family tradition Pépère had started.

It might be hard to reproduce now a sense of what a car would mean to a woman in her thirties who has spent the last ten years wiping bottoms, cooking meatloaf, and dusting the living room, only going out — even to the grocery store — if and when someone took you out. In fact, the grocery store wasn't a common outing for my mother, or for any of the other women in the neighborhood. The milkman made his rounds so early in the morning that on really frigid mornings you would find the bottles on the step, a little neck of frozen milk pushed up through the bottle's throat, that narrow column of frozen milk wearing the paper caps that had once fitted into the bottle's mouth. Later in the day, when the daddies had all gone to work, Pat Foley, the Cushman baker would come by with his huge basket of bread and cakes and cookies. Pat knew I loved a particular golden cake with toothachingly sweet white frosting, all shaggy with shredded coconut. If one of those were available, he'd tuck it in the basket and carry it to the door to see if he and I could persuade my mother that day. Eggs, dry cleaning, scissors sharpening, the Fuller Brush man with his vacuum cleaner bags and brushes, and in summer, ice cream and frozen lemonade; all of these vendors had their regular routes to sell door-to-door to the homebound mothers. For the rest of the groceries, my mother would phone Irene Boulanger at the market right across from Interstate Firebrick, my father's business. Irene would box up the order for my father and when he stopped to get it on his way home, Irene would slip in the refrigerated items and the meat she'd cut herself.

Such service may sound dreamlike to us now but consider the passivity of it. Like a sea anemone that waits for the right food to happen by, or goes hungry. By contrast, a car meant freedom, flexibility, choices. But I wonder, if staying home, no-wife-of-mine-will-ever-work has been a misty childhood dream, is it hard to admit to yourself that you can't stand all this staying home, that you actually loved going to work? Craved the interaction with other adults, the chance to showcase your own competencies.

My mother started back to work by way of pitching in. When I think about some of the assumptions my parents based life-changing decisions on, I have to wonder what I'm doing now that's just as misguided. My father's business was refractories: fireproof materials used to line boilers and kilns. Though he was supporting a family of six on it, it's dirty dangerous work. The bread-and-butter of the business is to rip out and replace the linings of plant furnaces. One day one of Dad's workers climbed into a furnace that was supposed to be shut down, but someone had made a mistake. Of course, Frank realized the mistake almost instantaneously. Horror-struck my father saw the flames licking out all around the man's body as Frank, a big man, struggled to wriggle back out. Frank survived, actually not even badly burned, but it set my father thinking. His expectation was his sons would one day want to take over his business; on the basis of that expectation, he decided that he ought to look for safer work.

Dad chose furniture. Later when he found out how ruthless and cutthroat the furniture business can be, he was rueful about selecting furniture over refractories because he'd thought of it as "cleaner." His plan was to run both businesses, at least until he could get the furniture store on its feet. He leased the old Gil Motors building in Arctic for a furniture showroom and borrowed from the Gelineau family corporation to get started. My mother went to work for the furniture store as combination accountant, buyer, and salesperson. We kids started summer day camp. Even Janine, who was only four.

Initially, in some ways I think they were happier. My mother named the store the Guild House. She liked the play on words with my father's name and the implication of fine craftsmanship. There were buyers' trips to furniture shows in New York City — very near to a vacation for just the two of them. Mrs. King and her poodle would move in with us kids for days at a time; she'd make us crêpes for breakfast, then there would be presents for each of us when Mom and Dad came home. But let's be realistic: they were in a Mixmaster — running two businesses, including a retail store open Saturdays and Thursday nights. And with family for your creditors. Money problems were a constant pressure and not a problem my parents ever handled well. Their experiences of money growing up had been just too widely different for them to agree, or even understand one another's positions very clearly. The fighting escalated — sometimes physical as well as verbal — and it wasn't long until the drinking became the accelerant poured over everything. Our lives became a conflagration but not one you could call out for help with. Some things are family things, our mother told us. They stay within the family. Decades have passed and still I've never told my closest friends, my own children, half the things I saw and heard.

Who among us has not been wounded by history, the immutable past we inherit, even the events and motivations we might burn to reject? Yes, especially those parts, the unquiet histories the unfiltered air our lungs must inhale. The unquiet histories as pervasive as air.

By the osmosis of hearing place names American children absorb an English that is deeply inflected with an element of the musicality of the hundreds of languages spoken by the indigenous populations: Mashpee, Narragansett, Misquamicut, Massachusetts, Connecticut, Meshanticut, Sockanosset, Apponaug, Weekapaug: the list goes on even just in my little childhood corner of the nation. The landscape itself has more than one way of passing on memory.

The day camp my siblings and I attended for five or six summers as the decade turned into the sixties was called Ok-wa-nessett, which so far as I know was an invented word intended to sound Native American, by way of suggesting its woodsy setting. Of course, a regimented day camp was no wilderness adventure, but children could and did find ways at Ok-wa-nessett to access the natural world, their true home.

Was I nine or ten, maybe eleven? Could have been any or all of those summers. I've slipped away from my group, the Big Sioux, and gone off into the woods alone. Skirting regulations was not something the rule-adhering parochial school girl did very often and so it was easy for me to convince my counselor I had forgotten something in our unit's tent and needed to go back for it. I likely even got what I'd said I'd come for but what I didn't do was to return directly to my group. I was off the trails, in the soft duff of the forest floor, at the marshy edge of the brook that fed the camp pond, hunting frogs. I loved the look and the smell of sunlight filtered through the oak, the maple, the sassafras; I loved the maidenhair ferns nodding from no more than the whisper of a disturbance I made moving past them. The quiet.

I wanted the fierce attention it takes to find the green-patterned frog in the green-patterned woodland floor, the absorption required to get close enough for my hand to suddenly cover that cool otherness, the way my voice cooing, a stroking finger could sometimes soothe the panic, the throbbing throat. And the silken, evaporating brush strokes the frog's body made in the water when I released it, its long-fingered legs thrusting, thrusting.

❖

My first weeks of elementary school, I was terrified of the nuns, swathed in black broadcloth, with that heavy wooden rosary swinging from their waist. It might have been the very first day that I spilled my little carton of milk as we sat eating our bagged lunches at our desks. Sister Mary Joseph swooped down the aisle, likely just to be helpful to me, but in my mind, I had been spotted by some hovering, raven-black predator, now diving toward me. I came so unglued with fright that, to his disgust, my brother was summoned from his own classroom to try to calm me.

I've already said what delighted me most about beginning first grade was the hefty hardbound reader I carried home proudly and read that night, finding the next day to my profound disappointment that it was our reader for the year. Fortunately, the Pontiac Free Library was in walking distance and in those days, mothers felt comfortable letting their children walk to the corner store to buy bread and milk, or to the library to take out their weekly allotment of books.

From the age of nine I thought of myself as destined to be a writer. In fourth grade that meant I pictured myself a Carolyn Keene, dreaming up a Nancy Drew series of my own. At St. Joseph's we were required to memorize a few poems — old chestnuts like Longfellow's "Paul Revere's Ride." Perhaps I remember that one most clearly because the lines were in the rhythm of a rapidly cantering horse: "Listen, my children, and you shall hear / Of the midnight ride of Paul Revere, / On the eighteen of April, in Seventy-five; / Hardly a man is now alive / Who remembers that famous day and year." I'm not at all sure I understood genre, that there was a difference of kind between the poem stories and the prose stories. It didn't seem to me something I needed to choose between.

A dreamy, bookish child, when my chores were done my mother would routinely shoo me out of the house to get fresh air and exercise, but often as not I absorbed my fresh air under a tree with an open book in my lap. And from an early age I entertained myself composing descriptions and small stories in my mind.

My Mémère was widowed relatively young, especially relative to the long life she still had ahead of her (Pépère died quietly in his sleep at the age of 70 when I was 8 years old; Mémère lived on to nearly reach her 103rd birthday). Valeda's sister Yvonne and her brother Oscar had both also been widowed by then and those three siblings moved in together. Through much of my childhood they spent the warm weather months in Aunt Yvonne's Rhode Island home and cold weather in Mémère's Florida house. Mémère would cook, Aunt Yvonne clean, and Uncle Oscar handled the yard. Uncle Oscar was a rosarian, one of the panel who helped to determine the All-American rose selections each year and I was one of the few of the grandchild generation not put off by the well-rotted horse manure he fertilized his roses with. To me, that just added to the allure.

Under Uncle Oscar's tutelage, my parents planted Jackson & Perkins tea roses the length of the fence circling our backyard, and one of my private pleasures was to describe to myself the exquisite colors of the blossoms, with two of my favorites being the buttercream yellows and pale pinks of the Peace — like a soft sunset on a stem — and the mysteriously black-red velvet of the Mirandy.

Most often my parents fought one another, not the external pressures crushing them, not the alcohol. Wild, passionate, wall-banging, crockery-flying arguments. In the aftermath, Dad would put doors back on their jambs and Mom would sweep up the broken plates or picture frames, but we needed to bring in Outsiders to repair the torn-out phone lines and replace the door locks stuffed with broken toothpicks. Of course, the phone lines had been torn out to begin with to keep Outsiders out there. The repairmen never said a word. That heavy silence of civility.

It's not the repairmen that I blame. My parents didn't drown without waving to shore but their signaling was ambivalent and in those days, the "lifeguards" didn't want to humiliate respectable victims by effecting public rescues if they didn't have to. If you were capable of keeping up appearances, everyone supported you in maintaining the fiction. My mother did go to a doctor — in fact, she went to several. To a man they told her she was depressed and gave her Valium to wash down with her Scotch. Then she'd draw the blinds and sink into uninterruptible sleep.

Like any infant, the cotyledon — that silver filament of root and sleek, green pseudoleaves that first emerge from a seed — suggests the possibility it could still become anything.

As a sixth grader, I was helping my mother with dinner preparations in the kitchen one day when she said to me, "Gibby will finish eighth grade this year and be moving on to high school. We're going to send him to Bishop Hendrickson High School. That will cost a lot of money, and so your father and I have decided to take you out of St. Joseph's School at the end of this year and next September you'll be going to the public school instead. A good education is more important for a boy than it is for a girl."

The moment is indelible in my mind, standing by the stove waiting while my mother ladled dinner onto plates for me to ferry to the table, her comment to me seemingly almost an afterthought to her. As if she were passing on neutral information. The roar in my ears when I hear those words repeat has never entirely gone away.

My two years at Cranston West Junior-Senior High School were a nightmare. In these days of social media, the bullying often starts earlier now, but then seventh and eighth grades were prime mean-girl years, and what better target than the meek Catholic school outsider who didn't know enough not to leap respectfully to her feet to answer the teacher when called on? Seventh-grade girls, you understand, are piranhas and here I was, live bait. Only my time each summer at camp gave the slightest credence to my mother's contention that the problem was not me but them. All summer, every summer at Ok-wa-nessett I was comfortably and ordinarily popular. It might well not be an exaggeration to say it saved my life.

I bring it up to say who knows what source poetry came from? Did the pressures of being the target of bullying contribute? Whatever the source and inspiration, I was visited by my first poem as I gazed out the open door to a bank of ornamental grass while daydreaming in music class at Cranston West. I can reproduce all but one word of that little proto-poem from memory to this day, and even the one word I'm unsure of, the rhythm of it I know for certain:

> Tufts *(or shocks or something one syllable)* of grass stood
> stretching to the sky
> begging for rain
>
> the ghost of a breeze sprung up
> to ripple the grass into waves
> of rain-starved gold
>
> the ghost passed on
> the grass stretched back
> begging for rain

Melodramatic, surely, but I was thirteen so it seems to me what distinguishes this little attempt is the focus on sound rather than teenage angst, with stanza one and three reenacting stasis, while stanza two ripples. There in music class, it was the music of language that drew me to poetry.

Birth is a normal process and like any animal, the mare, in the vast majority of instances, gives birth unaided without incident. But the mare owner with a hefty investment of funds, and more importantly, emotion, can't risk that small percentage of times in which their presence might have been of some use had they been there. That's the rationale for foal watch, but if I were to be honest about the thing, I would have to admit to the awe. The pure wish to be present for the first moment that fish-fetus transforms to impossibly new land creature.

Being there can be more complicated than it sounds. Labor happens quickly in the mare. Powerful waves of contractions expel the foal, often in no more than ten or fifteen minutes from the time the water breaks to the time the shimmering hind legs slip free of the vulva's lip. And like their fellow mammals, the human, most mares give birth in the early morning hours so foal watch is chiefly a nocturnal process, an activity of the set-apart time of darkness.

My foal watch station is a bed in the barn aisle just outside the stall of the mare due to foal. A light burns over her stall, a bit of an inconvenience for us both but a better solution than introducing light suddenly when the birth is upon us. The Sheltie curled at the foot of my double-decker sleeping bags makes a companionable foot warmer. All in all, it could be quite restful if it weren't for the anticipation.

Foal watch is heavy anticipation, anticipation unleavened with fear. When you're the one the pregnancy inhabits, the intensity of your desire for the moment of birth to come is balanced by the intensity of your fear that it will come. Rationally you know there's only one way out of this but emotionally you find yourself slipping into prayer, and the prayer often calls for some god somewhere to invent a new way out of the situation for your special instance.

The mare suffers no such reflections. She dozes or paces the stall, the rustle of the straw is punctuated with arrhythmic thumps as she occasionally swats an annoyed foot toward her twitching abdomen: prelabor, or just another of the weeks of practice contractions which tone the muscles for the real event? Your ears strain to interpret every footfall. The books tell you once the muscles have relaxed over the tailhead, the vulva has slackened, and waxy exudate has formed on the teats, that labor should be imminent, but experience tells you this can go on for days, every delivery unique, individual. Dawn comes and it's necessary to get up and go about your responsibilities with only half an eye and an ear trained on the mare instead of the whole of your senses and attention. You must return the most of yourself to the everyday. But generally, that day passes without incident and you return, reimmerse in foal watch, like some ritual that needs to be performed a requisite number of times before the holy event can take place.

The horses attend respectfully to the birth when it comes. They wake to the sharp smell of amniotic fluid as the waters break and wait quietly, attentively in their stalls, ears pricked toward the birthing stall. Sometimes the foaling mare lies down before the water breaks, sometimes just after, but the normal position for the mare at delivery is flat on her side, legs extended and trembling with the effort. I wonder specifically about women. What is the normal position in which women give birth? I have given birth twice out of my own body, and yet so acculturated has the process become that I cannot figure it clearly. How would I have given birth if the hospital had not put me in a bed? There's a lot to be said for squatting, legs wide, pelvis spread to the utmost and gravity lending a hand. But how to support your back? How to catch the baby? Lean against a tree? Bend over the engorged, contracting abdomen and catch the crowning head with your own hands? We don't really want to do this alone, do we? Does the clumsiness of birthing alone mark the human as a social animal?

We live so much of the rest of our lives cerebrally that the process of reproduction is chewy by contrast, sustainingly bodily. At no other time do you live more *in* your body, more *embodied* than those nine months of pregnancy. And yet, paradoxically, never are you less in control of your body, never is your body less your own than during labor and delivery. You can neither decide to give birth nor control it once it has begun. Birth is not something that you or the baby does. It is a process that is done *to* you both, some undeterrable force that boils up out of the interaction of your bodies together. A certain critical mass is reached and birth happens, like a storm out of the right mix of meteorologic conditions. It is no more under the influence of your consciousness than a hurricane is.

How often have men figured women as having the power of childbirth, and claimed powers to themselves — from art to war — as their equivalency to women's power of childbirth? And women have parroted that language back. Who could blame us, few as the powers attributed to us have been? But it is not power a woman has in childbirth. It is humility, but the language doesn't yet contain a word that would mean humility electrified, energized, and interconnected in the sense of the emotion a woman who has just been delivered of her newborn feels. Birth embeds you in life and death; you are in connection not in control.

The foal's shape presents a riskier candidate for the birth canal than a human baby's does. The baby is all globular surfaces, rounded and nonthreatening to the mother's inner surfaces; the foal, by contrast, is serpentine, branching, and tipped by tiny hooves. Packaged well, delivery is possible, and so the foal comes packaged, still cased in the caul. A bubble of fluid at the front of the amnion eases the way, cushioning the forefeet, which will emerge first. Ingeniously, the hooves are slippered in little pads of spongy material called eponychium intended only for this journey; the pads are lost in the neonate's first efforts to rise. One foreleg emerges, then the next, offset to help the shoulders pass the pelvis. By the time the knees are visible the little muzzle can be seen beneath the silver membrane of the caul. The long wedge of the head takes time to pass because at this point the mare has her hardest work to accomplish, pushing the foal's shoulders over the lip of her own pelvis. Shoulders past, the foal swishes to the rib cage in a small wash of fluids. A strong foal will already be batting about in its iridescent sac, tearing the caul, shaking free into air and light. The mare regroups and bears down. The hips pass and supple foal squirts from her, momentarily still as fluid as if it were yet fetal. The two rest together, placental blood pulsing the cord between them. The foal shakes, sneezes fluid, whinnies. Answering whinnies sound all up and down the barn aisle — high-pitched, curious — but it is the dam's deep tremolo to which the foal responds.

I saw things no child should see and yet it was not an inevitable spiral like bathwater down the drain. My mother had an adamantine will and on will alone would get through a workday, or drag herself up from sleep to fix our supper. Dinner on the table for her children was some kind of marker in her mind: if she was accomplishing that, she wasn't as bad as she believed the rumors about herself to be. As if it were a syllogism: the mother who provides supper every night cannot be a drunk, I provide dinner every night, therefore, I cannot be a drunk.

And there were lulls. Weeks, even months at a time when the family picture we presented to the world felt nearly the same at home. Routines would resume, the air was light, no glasses by the bed stand or bottles beneath the kitchen sink. One of the occasions my mother pulled herself together for most brilliantly was the bankruptcy.

The Guild House was a shark, a voracious feeder whose appetite for time and money and effort never slaked. Dad sold Interstate Firebrick and fed the proceeds and his energies full time into the furniture store. That tamped things down for a while but only for a while. The storeroom fire was the final weight on the wrong side of the balance scale. He was going under and the creditors he owed were his own family, his mother and his siblings. When hope was still alive that they could make it, the stress on my mother had been unbearable, but once the end became inevitable, she calmed. She'd been poor before. What mattered now was Dad.

He went back into refractories. The employee now, working for a man in Connecticut whom he had helped get going years before. Miraculously, the house we eventually bought in Connecticut was twice the house we'd had in Rhode Island — my mother's dream house. There on Valley View Drive, old haunts, old habits were substantially left behind.

The open and innocent lust of tulips: petals arc back in the lick of sunlight, exposing the sticky star mouth of the pistil in its garland of pollen-dusted anthers gesturing from their stalks.

May

The cunning violets, who laid low in last week's frost, unfurl now with the perfect purple rectitude of violets. A lithe butterfly rows the cumbersome extravagance of its white silk wings through the sun-thick air over constellations of dandelions.

On the hillsides, the feral apple trees froth out in bloom wherever the happenstance of scat has scattered them. The trees hold bridal blossoms in their gnarled arms like the body's own memory of its youth.

The move to Connecticut marked a significant improvement. I myself was coming off of a golden last summer at Ok-wa-nessett, where I had been elevated from camper to counselor-in-training and I was experiencing first love with Buzz, a sixteen-year-old counselor. We group-dated with all our friends from camp, including my brother Gib and his girlfriend. I rode to the top of the Rocky Point Amusement Park Ferris wheel with Buzz's arm around my shoulders as we looked out at the lights sparkling around Narraganset Bay. I had my first kiss from Buzz in the finished basement of one of our group of friends while the bunch of us slow danced to 45s on the record player. That September I felt ready to face life at Cranston West, mean girls or no, but I didn't have to. Instead, the Conncctioul school I transferred to was welcoming, the start to a fine high school experience.

And my mother's life improved. She took on a secretarial/office management job, my parents made new friends. Family life took on healthier rhythms.

It wasn't flawless. Gibby's high school graduation night was a classic of the family respectability dance, choreography we all knew in our bones. When Gibby was supposed to be in the music room of the high school suiting up and wisecracking with his friends, he was an ominously contained volcano of anger, waiting on the bench of the porch picnic table. All four of us kids were out there on the porch, showered, shined, and waiting. Mom was drunk and not dressed yet, her energies focused on fighting with Dad. The terms of the fight are inconsequential since their fights only infrequently centered on the real issues.

Now that my own children are grown and leaving home, I have more understanding of some of what might have pushed her into drinking on the evening her oldest was graduating from high school. Her sorrows would have been inchoate and nameless, blurred by the booze, but untamed by it. The loss of "her baby," the onrush of her own mortality, a litany of lost dreams and lost possibilities. Maybe even her own losses at Gibby's age.

We made it to graduation that night, kept up appearances, went on. And then in August, a week's vacation at the beach, all together as a family, was just the latest evidence of our strengthening expertise at normalcy.

We'd spent that week at Popponesset in Gramps and Nana's cottage. The final weekend of vacation, Mom and Dad had a wedding to attend in Washington, DC, and to our great surprise, they had suggested we should take both cars out to the Cape: they would leave Thursday afternoon and we kids could have two more beach days and solo home on Sunday in the station wagon. We were calving icebergs, breaking free, loose along the Atlantic, on our own. Parentless and glad as the heroes of some children's novel.

We'd expected to be back ahead of them but their car was already in the drive when we got there. Mom was upstairs in bed and sick enough to have Dad worried. Mom had felt alright even during the wedding ceremony but then she'd been hit — like a sudden flu — so instantaneous and insistent that they'd had to leave the reception early. After an uncomfortable night in the hotel, they'd headed home first thing in the morning. Now Dad was talking hospital.

I didn't have the slightest premonition. You could as soon have said to me, didn't it occur to you the sun might not come up tomorrow? Mom was burning up with fever, enough to endure the privacy invasion of having her oldest daughter sponge bathe her everywhere with isopropyl alcohol to cool her down while Dad phoned ahead to the hospital. That worried me, the gray look to her and the funereal sensation of seeing a helpless parent naked. But I was over that as soon as Dad called home with a diagnosis of pneumonia. Who doesn't know someone who's had pneumonia? The next day, Monday night when Dad got home from work, I went to the hospital with him for visiting hours. The idea was we kids would all take turns visiting and I went first.

Mom looked much better that Monday, sitting up in bed in her hospital johnny. Dad brought pajamas and a pretty robe from home, her slippers. I remember a relaxed visit. The one and only thing I can recall my mother saying to me was snapping at me exasperatedly when I couldn't figure out the hospital bed and folded her up by accidentally cranking the foot of the bed instead of the head. It was just one small hot bite of a remark in an otherwise pleasant hour, but it's the one damn thing I can remember. That, and that we waved goodbye to one another cheerily as we left the room.

But Tuesday Dad went in alone. And Wednesday. Thursday night Dad called to say he'd be spending the night there. Gibby stopped me at the door to my room as I was headed in to bed. "I know we haven't always gotten along," he groused, to cover his concern, "but she doesn't have to kick the bucket." I was stunned at how much smarter he was than me. I had been so firmly in denial.

In fact, Mom's temperature had spiked to 106 degrees way back on Tuesday, plummeting her into a coma. Nothing they'd done had brought the fever down and after days at that temperature, there really was no hope of any Marion coming back, even if they could have roused her from the coma.

No doubt with good intentions, my father had told her parents, her sisters and her brother not to come — she wouldn't know them anyway and it would "alarm the children." Alarm the children? That wake-up call came Friday morning. After a sleepless night at Mom's bedside, Dad drove home to have his breakfast with us, leaving Mom alone there in the ICU. Just about the time his car swung into our driveway, she drifted away, a drowning victim bound for the impenetrable deeps, leaving us behind, now and irretrievably, motherless, and free.

The allotment is brief — perhaps a single afternoon — each bloom upon the lilac a lantern of perfection: scent, color, texture, form. Still other springs even that hour rain comes to quench.

When my parents were married, they drove off on an auto-loop honeymoon — the de rigor–for-the-times Niagara Falls visit then on to Québec City, where my father used bravado and his mother tongue of Québécois to score a suite at the Château Frontenac, and finally they spent time at a cabin in Maine where my mother may have first realized the role fishing was going to take in her husband's life, if not directly her own.

On their way driving back to Rhode Island, they stopped there in Maine to buy a boxer puppy they named Dagmar after the woman *Life* magazine referred to in 1951 as "a national institution" and the *New York Times* described in her obituary decades later as "a dumb-as-a-fox blonde on one of television's first late-night shows."

When their first child, my brother, Gibby, arrived two days after their first anniversary, Dagmar the boxer apparently adjusted to the addition of the new baby, but when Gibby began to walk, the young dog's enthusiasm for trying to engage the toddler in play backfired on her. Concluding it was the baby or the dog, my parents rehomed Dagmar. In her new home, Dagmar became a show dog and eventually a champion boxer, so apparently, she landed where she belonged, but unfortunately for me, the Dagmar experience had soured my mother on any more dogs. It was not only that I couldn't have a horse on our quarter acre lot but even a dog was suspected of becoming too much trouble.

Like so many, I had fallen in love with collies through the TV show *Lassie* and pined for a dog of my own. Cousin Donna and her siblings had a blonde, mostly cocker spaniel named Ginger that I adored and lavished walks, petting, and grooming on at every opportunity, but Ginger lived in Massachusetts and I lived in Rhode Island, so that was an inadequate substitute for a dog of our own. The most burdensome pet my mother would agree to was a dime storm goldfish in its little globe-shaped bowl. Dime storm goldfish in an unaerated bowl filled with tap water have a very short lifespan. At the edge of our yard and "the field," my brothers and I fashioned a little graveyard with popsicle stick crosses for the golden deceased and eventually let go of the idea we would ever have a pet.

During the sixteen days between my mother's funeral and my "sweet sixteen" birthday, my father saw a classified ad for "Miniature Collie" puppies. Tiny classified ads don't happen to catch your eye as you flip through the paper, so clearly my father had decided to look for a puppy for me. Knowing my obsession with Lassie, and the size of our yard, "Mini-Collie" sounded perfect to him. One evening in the week before my birthday, my dad asked if I wanted to go for a ride with him. We were all sticking close to one another, keeping one another company by unspoken agreement, so I presumed he had an errand and would appreciate having someone ride along. I thought this right up until the moment I caught sight of the Sheltie Puppies for sale sign on the fenced backyard of the house we pulled up to.

It was an inspired gift. Shetland Sheepdogs are not actually Collies selectively bred down to be tiny, but rather the breed developed on the Shetland Islands independently from other Collies but from the same root stock. Like Border Collies, Shelties are whip-smart, and like Shetland ponies (and Shetland sheep), Shelties are of compact size. My first Sheltie, Missy — a black with white and tan markings (a tri in Sheltie parlance) — was demure, self-possessed, and brilliant — the perfect soulmate for an animal-crazy and bereft teenager.

The day of my sixteenth birthday my father came out of the house from the screened-in porch to where I was playing with my puppy in the grass.

"Let's go for a ride," he said, jingling the car keys. He meant, "time for you to learn to drive now that you're sixteen. Time to get on with life." I tried to avoid, delay, refuse, but my father recognized it for what it was — the phlegmatic capitulation to the sense of aimlessness grief can bring — and was having none of that.

Now getting therapy to help a family navigate a loss such as the one we all had suffered would be normal and acceptable, but in 1966, therapy was what one did if one failed to recover on their own. We got on with it. Less than a month after we had suddenly become motherless, Gib left home to begin college. The new school year began for the newly turned sixteen-year-old, the thirteen-year-old, and the eleven-year-old. Our supermarket was running a promotion that year where your purchases could earn a volume of the *Women's Day Encyclopedia of*

Cookery each week. Week by week, Dad brought a volume home until he had the complete set, and armed with that advice, he proceeded to teach himself to cook.

The loss would hit you in unguarded moments — I remember grabbing six forks as usual one night as I set the table for dinner . . . and then sadly putting Mommy's and Gibby's forks back in the drawer. One day in English class, we read (or did I only come across it in our anthology on our way to what the class was reading?) Edna St. Vincent Millay's "Lament."

> Listen, children:
> Your father is dead.
> From his old coats
> I'll make you little jackets;
> I'll make you little trousers
> From his old pants.
> There'll be in his pockets
> Things he used to put there,
> Keys and pennies
> Covered with tobacco;
> Dan shall have the pennies
> To save in his bank;
> Anne shall have the keys
> To make a pretty noise with.
> Life must go on,
> And the dead be forgotten;
> Life must go on,
> Though good men die;
> Anne, eat your breakfast;
> Dan, take your medicine;
> Life must go on;
> I forget just why.

The final couplet echoed in my mind for years. The poem was an enormous comfort to me. Others had been where I was and come through.

In his poem, "The Pardon," the poet Richard Wilbur said, "I dreamt the past was never past redeeming." He wrote this far enough back in the twentieth century that we still did not routinely imagine ourselves, or our grandchildren, outliving history.

The direst of the warnings now say we have just eighteen months from when I'm writing this to take meaningful action or the natural consequences of the carbon load we are releasing will push the delicate balance upon which our atmosphere depends too far over the line for us to reverse. Won't it already be eighteen months from now when you are reading this? Is there any possibility then of you reading it? Have we already outlived history?

If we humans take no meaningful action in time, yet do manage to find a way to preserve some portion of the species, won't those survivors live in a wholly built environment, an environmental fortress? Even with no space ship involved, those survivors will be living on an entirely different planet. In that utterly altered world, won't the millennia of our collective history, literature, culture have become unintelligible? In a world bereft of the referents like seasons, rainbows, gardens, forests, etcetera that then will no longer exist for the humans of that day to experience, how will we be intelligible to any descendants we might technically have? Will it still be history then, or some kind of restart that is in no way a resumption?

What Wilbur seems to have meant was something along the line that we have imagined our lives to begin with, and thus could reimagine them as well, revise the narratives we tell ourselves and others to produce that comforting sense of self that allows us to feel at least some measure of *at home* within our knowledge of our own mortality. That both the conscious and the unconscious minds shape and reshape that ever-evolving narrative, fecund thus with the potential to invent redemption.

But what cannot be escaped is that that sprite spirit is manifested within a corporeal body, a body remorselessly dependent upon the material world. Flesh is tied to Earth, dust to dust, and what we do unto the Earth, we do unto ourselves.

That material world lives within a present that can be pushed beyond salvation by a profligate past. Redemptive and pernicious as imagination can be, imagination alone will not suffice.

One Sunday drive when childhood was still simple, before problems had multiplied, we rode through the University of Rhode Island campus with my father pointing out places he had lived or had classes or adventures. The story I remember best was about how he and his fraternity brothers had kept a ram, the school mascot, in the cellar of the fraternity house but, more than the specifics of any of my father's reminiscences, I was impressed with the tree-lined streets, the young people strolling, and the buildings dedicated to learning. As I sat in the front between my two parents, I could sense the affection in my father's voice for the memory of what it was to be coming of age on a comfortable campus before the war. Not that he spoke of it or that I had any awareness then but in his memory there had to have been the contrast between his first three years of college life, that time before interrupting his senior year to join up with the army and endure all he experienced during World War II. So there was the warmth of his nostalgia for a time of lost innocence and freedom in my father's voice, but also, I could feel the palpable hunger of my mother for a past that had never been available to her. About this time her much-younger youngest sister Patricia was a student on full scholarship at Albertus Magnus College in New Haven, Connecticut, whereas my mother, the oldest in the family, had had to use her sterling high school record to graduate high school early and help support the family. College had not been an option. I felt both a powerful draw to that landscape of the campus and the strong yearning from both of my parents for the life that landscape seemed to promise. I knew with certainty from that day that I would go to college.

That said, my knowledge about college, the differences in schools, the process of acceptance and financing, my access to information about those things never really expanded much beyond the little drive through the URI campus as a child. When the time came that I was making decisions on where to apply to college, my mother had been dead just a year. I thought college tuition sticker prices were immutable. I could see there were four of us children and my dad still struggling to be all things to all of us. In my mind, my state university was my only option. I was aware that with my grades and my SAT scores, I would be accepted so I never even applied anywhere else.

Eventually I came to understand my high school's guidance program could have provided a lot more help than what they did, that that had been an important juncture at which other lives could have unfolded for me but given the happiness I have had, given the two lifelong friends I made there, and the way that that choice led to the man I would marry, how could there be anything like regret?

Horses inhabit their lives unselfconsciously. Surely that's the root of their ease: the way they inhabit their lives completely because of their lack of any awareness of being alive. They escape observing themselves, judging themselves, calibrating worth. They learn, they have emotions, but their emotions are unsullied by self-regard.

Of course, all other-than-human animals have this quality but we find it most remarkable among those species most like ourselves, who we are most able to live among. Cats have this in abundance but something about the size of horses in relationship to us, the fact that we can actually be carried off with them on their backs, our bodies to a glorious degree melding with theirs, gives a presence and a gravitas that it does not seem to me domestic cats can equal. Had I the opportunity to live among giraffes, or elephants, or gorillas, I'm sure they would provide a similar respite from our awareness of self, holy opportunities to live wholly, mindful, and content in the moment.

❖

How can we not fail? We who can access continents and centuries of knowing? Cultures, languages, epistemological systems of all kinds . . . what is the correct amount to know, now that the concept of renaissance has imploded under the weight of all that we can learn? Is it better to be peripatetic and speak six languages, or know one tract of land with the intimacy of an ant? Who decides "better"?

Though he doted on his grandchildren, and we were thus shielded from that side of his personality, my Irish grandfather was a hard man who could hold fast to the narrow opinions the straited circumstances of his youth had forged in him. Both of my mother's parents came to love my father dearly, but on the night my parents were engaged, my Dad waited in the kitchen while his new fiancée went into the living room to tell her father the news. Seeing his daughter coming into the room, Gramps made no effort to modulate his voice when he preempted her announcement with a gruff, "So you're going to marry the damn Frenchman?" In Gramps's mind his oldest daughter should only have been considering Irish Catholics. A measure of how constricted his view of *us* and *them* was.

One would think that a man who had grown up in an occupied country, a country he was forced out of for political reasons, a man who arrived on the shores of a new land where he had just his wits and his strength to make his way with, who had faced NINA placards, which even marginally literate Irish immigrants knew signified No Irish Need Apply, one might think such a history would incline one to empathize with other groups suppressed and despised for equally unfair and capricious reasons, but in fact such circumstances were at least as likely to inspire a fierce sense of competition for what little slice of the pie was left over for those in the lower registers. The only heated argument I ever heard my parents have on any topic outside of their own marriage erupted at the dinner table one night when my mother advanced an opinion she'd inherited from her father that "separate but equal" was sound social policy.

My father, who'd seen blatant racism at work when he joined the Army halfway through his senior year of college and was sent south for training, knew the inequality that self-serving formulation sought to excuse. On leave in town he would try to step off the sidewalk and provide room for the black mother and her children, or the black women heading home from their day jobs, but of course, he was actually mostly making things harder for them because they could not have a white man stepping politely off the curb to let them pass on the sidewalk, however much he might have wanted that. That night at our supper table our father angrily dissected and demolished my mother's arguments, making clear there was nothing "equal" about the separations of American society.

I was struck that my two parents could be so far apart on issues of how community ought to work. Based on our Kentucky-born nuns teaching that we were all God's children, I was certain my father was right and my mother wrong. There in suburban Cranston (and West Warwick where my school and my day camp were), there were no real-world opportunities to try out any of those theories — there was not a single child I knew growing up in my neighborhood, my school, my church, my Brownie troop, my camp who was not white like me. Nothing in my experience to question the nuns' assurance that Jesus loves us all the same. Like a virus that can be unseen but virulent, that insidious white privilege of not needing to think about race.

> One has to be able at every moment to place one's hand on the earth like the first human being.
> — Rilke
> *Letters on Cézanne*

For years I had that remark of Rilke's pinned over my writing desk. I can't remember how I found the quote, only that it came to me free-floating, out of the context that had produced it, and that the words struck me powerfully as if Rilke had spoken for me a long-held aesthetic goal I had never actually articulated to myself. Not just a goal for art, but a way of being alive to one's own life. A credo.

The redbud we planted the spring the first grandchild had been born roots into the earth's heart, drinks the melody there until her branches burst into fuchsia song.

June

Summer surges out of the detritus of spring. Whereas spring implied to us she could turn death into life — the hellebores and crocuses splitting the bare, winter-scalded earth with the silken flags of their petals — summer says, the peonies scatter their voluptuousness among the shriveled spears of last month's daffodils, roses open out beside the dimmed lanterns of lilac blossoms — death intermixed with life, as it always is, feeding one another.

At college orientation they issued us freshman beanies and explained parietal hours to us. The beanies a few of us even wore to the Orientation barbeque but "lost" well before classes convened. As to curfew, for the most part we signed in and out dutifully, evading the deadline no more egregiously than any other class for perhaps a semester, but this was the tumultuous year of 1968, and the ground was already crumbling beneath the house mothers' feet. The times they were a-changin'.

Inevitably gentile regulations like *male visitors allowed only in the lounge* were obliterated and as a practical matter dorm councils were working out roommate and bathroom protocols for all the opposite sex visitors up in the bedrooms. I took my own advantage of shifting standards by moving my dog, Missy, in.

During the four years I was at the University of Connecticut, I studied American literature with the Willa Cather scholar William Curtin; British poetry with Oxford-educated South African Murray Biggs; Black Mountain Poets with the Charles Olson acolyte George Butterick (Olson himself was a visiting professor at UConn during my freshman year but his health was already broken and he died in New York hospital in the middle of my sophomore year. I certainly never met him); and the one workshop I ever took as an undergraduate — workshops still being something of a new idea for college curriculum — was with Marcella Spann, who had visited Ezra Pound while he was at St. Elizabeth's, compiling with Pound the anthology *Confucius to Cummings*. Spann assigned us Pound's *ABC of Reading* and did her best to run the workshop as if we were students of an offshoot of the Ezuversity. It was only later that I learned the larger context of who Ezra Pound was.

❖

What dangerous fictions are we telling ourselves now? Of course, there is not a single one, but there is a single one with the potential to swamp all others.

Early in the process of writing what became this book, I wrote to a friend to express my admiration for a poem of his that had appeared in the Academy of American Poets' daily column. We had a brief exchange, both describing our personal lives as going very well while bemoaning our anguish over the cultural and political state of affairs at a national level. The friend recommended a book he had read recently that had helped to coalesce his thinking on some aspects of this. *The Great Derangement* by Amitav Ghosh.

Months passed and I finally got ahold at the same time of both the book and enough time to read it. What I had expected was a book about the climate emergency. It is that but told from the point of view of a novelist, which is to say Ghosh's concern is language and form and the way a strong cultural narrative can derange our thinking. In other words, how the crap we tell ourselves about the nature of things can blind us to the actual nature of things.

I certainly recommend Ghosh's own explication of his ideas, but as I understand it, Ghosh is theorizing that an explanation for why we seem so unable to wrap our heads around the urgency of what our actions are doing to the planet is because for centuries now we have been lulled into an "everyday" understanding of world events and even cosmology and thus seem incapable of processing warnings of "catastrophe" as anything other than primitive thinking that will be disproved and needn't worry us.

Ghosh's argument is that until the time of the Enlightenment, humans understood the world as unpredictable — your children weren't all going to live, a hailstorm that would flatten the crop your winter survival depended on was as likely as a sunny afternoon, any new day could conceal the life-altering calamity you had not yet even imagined — but with the Enlightenment came a new way of viewing the world, in which humans began to exert what felt to us like influence. Bit by bit, knowledge was uncovered, control (or at least the illusion of control) increased. Ghosh points to Stephen Jay Gould's study of the competing geologic theories of catastrophism and gradualism, *Time's Arrow, Time's Cycle*: "In Gould's telling of the story, the catastrophist recounting of the earth's history is exemplified by Thomas Burnet's *Sacred Theory of the Earth* (1609), in which the narrative turns on events of 'unrepeatable uniqueness.' As opposed to this, the gradualist approach, championed by James Hutton (1726–1797) and Charles Lyell (1797–1875), privileges slow processes that unfold over time at even, predictable rates. The central credo in this doctrine . . . to put it simply: 'Nature does not make leaps'" (Ghosh 19–20). The gradualist approach supplanted the catastrophic through modernity's highly successful mode of labeling other forms of knowledge primitive and obsolete. This is Ghosh quoting Gould quoting Lyell: "'In an early stage of advancement, when a great number of natural appearances are unintelligible, an eclipse, an earthquake, a flood, or the approach of a comet, with many other occurrences afterwards found to belong to the regular course of events, are regarded as prodigies. The same delusion prevails as to moral phenomena, and many of these are ascribed to the intervention of demons, ghosts, witches, and other immaterial and supernatural agents'" (20). Gould's conclusion, Ghosh's conclusion, the twenty-first-century scientific consensus is a new humility. We don't have all the answers. Nature appears to continue to insist on its allegiance to *both* process and leaping, gradualism and catastrophe. We're not as smart as we've been acting as if we are. Picture a History of Unintended Consequences. Actually, we all have front-row seats to the unfolding of just such an episode now.

I have already said in these pages, nature will be nature, nature will not save us. We understand that history — personal, national, global, cosmic — is an artifact shaped out of that other human construct, language. It's a narrative imposed by the human mind by means of language to give shape to the shapelessness. Ghosh refers to these narratives as *a regime of thought and practice*. That we implement, put practice to our thought, is crucial, of course. His point is that the narrative that has served us these past three centuries from the Enlightenment until recently is now locking us into a collision course with *what is*. Though the writer may utilize tropes of nature in the pursuit of metaphor and allegory, nature itself is profoundly neither metaphoric nor allegorical. Nature is outside of language, ineluctably real. Though we may absorb the narratives we construct to shape and add a sense of meaning to our lives to such an extent that we come to think of them as "true," invisible even in our construction of our narratives as "natural," but to the extent that we are wrong or blind about any of that, the artificiality of our compositions will out. Melting ice caps and their consequences are profoundly uninfluenced by human narratives of wistful hopefulness.

Truth telling is the most impossible of language's uses to achieve . . . and yet, the attempt to do so anyway, is language's principal nobility.

❖

The first decision I made about this book was the form. My thought was that though it was prose I intended to shape the book along similar principles to what I had learned from writing my book-length poetic sequence *Appetite for the Divine* some decades earlier. Like that earlier book, I wanted this book to employ both formal shaping and intuitive leaps simultaneously. I wanted prose to handle time more as lyric does than as narrative tends to, favoring synchronicity over chronology. I am grateful for Ghosh's articulation of the role of narrative in our derangement on two accounts. For the way his analysis so neatly provides a theoretical underpinning to the form I came to instinctively (or if not through instinct than at least through poetry) — a form that both proceeds and leaps — and for the way his book works to rearticulate the lesson we know but are always purposefully forgetting: the imperfect alignment between the world as it is and the glorious but inadequate construct through which we understand and manipulate that world — language. We blur our memory of that disconnect as a matter of course because it is impractical in the day-to-day of ordinary life to keep calibrating the gap, but rising seas, burning forests, voracious storms, melting glaciers, cataclysm great and small are insisting now on a large-scale recalibration of the narratives we tell ourselves, and the world as it is.

Perhaps a week into my freshman year, I spotted a classified ad in the student newspaper for riding lessons at the Horse Barn down in the ag school and eagerly followed up on it. The University of Connecticut at the time was one of four land grant New England colleges whose ag schools had a Morgan horse breeding program through which they raised their own stock for their equine programs.

My riding instructor encouraged me with the idea that being a beginner at eighteen was a good thing in that I had no bad habits in need of correcting. During my years at UConn, I took twice-weekly lessons and enough equine classes that it could have qualified as my minor if my adviser had let me. Animal studies minor was not considered appropriate for an English major and so my official minor became education. I had completed sufficient ed classes during the semesters when I had flirted with the idea of becoming a high school English teacher, before admitting to myself that I would be chickening out before I had begun by following that path. What I wanted to do was write, and I recognized that if I went into teaching I would siphon off my energies into teaching and never devote the necessary time to writing. To prevent such self-sabotage, I switched my major from English education back to English.

My riding lessons went on in the summer as well as during the academic year, and one thing I learned from driving from our suburban home in South Windsor to the much more agricultural environs of Storrs, Connecticut, was a recognition of how the tension in my body relaxed the farther I got from traffic and the closer I got to the barn. I came to realize how deeply attuned I was to being in nature, and in the company of the self-possession of the horses. Which is how I came to the knowledge that even though I understood aspiring writers were supposed to go to New York City, I knew viscerally and with complete certainty that I was not equipped to flourish there.

What I did not have during those four university years was any kind of attention from a poet professor who could mentor me or pass on the slightest information about the literary and publishing world in the United States. I was exposed to ideas about poetry, particularly the ideas of Pound and Olson, but I was clueless about how one became a writer, other than a vague idea that if you wanted to become a writer, moving to New York City was the sensible first step, but a step I understood as closed to me. The only poet role models I was introduced to who seemed to bear any resemblance to my own situation were Emily Dickinson (because she was an American woman and so few women came up in the reading we were exposed to) and Robert Frost (because he lived in a rural, New England setting). Yes, I had heard of Sylvia Plath, and was wowed by the solar plexus punch of her poems but an expatriate moody suicide was no role model for the life of a poet I hoped to lead. By contrast, Frost's literary success while living on a hardscrabble farm encouraged me.

With year-round twice-weekly lessons I was able to progress rapidly and began to be a rider with skills enough to be helpful to the horse. I was able to arrange an independent study one semester working UC Charity, a valued young mare from the university breeding program who was a little too sensitive to blossom being trained in a group by a variety of marginally experienced riders (which, banking on the native intelligence and patience of Morgans, is the way the majority of their young stock learned, horses and riders progressing together in a group in the ring under the instructor's direction). That semester I earned college credit for working with Charity, I would start my day at the Horse Barn in a one-on-one session with the young mare and then slip into my literature classes with a dog or two at my heels and a pair of hunt boots slung over my shoulder.

That summer I skipped Woodstock on purpose — crowds made me claustrophobic — but when I heard the ads on the radio for this rock festival in upstate New York I encouraged my boyfriend to go. He and his buddies paid for tickets by mail, got as far as the shoulder of Route 17, and tried to hike in but were beaten back by the chaos and never made it to the site.

I had no regret at missing the party but when Joni sang, *We've got to get ourselves back*, the garden was real to me, I felt the longing, the need.

❖

They say if you remember the sixties, you weren't really there. I was on the verge of there.

With one roach-worth of a small exception, I did no drugs at all, but my boyfriend for a time was one of the most active dealers on campus. He took ironic pleasure in the fact that his abstemious girlfriend could eyeball a baggy of weed and judge when it held an ounce as accurately as his scale, he cross-legged on the floor measuring out his product, me propped against the wall on his bed, studying.

How innocent it all seemed. Who among his customers did not know the location of his little refrigerator where he kept the speed, and yet they knocked on the door and paid him for the pills they would use to pull their all-nighter or enjoy their Saturday night.

Once I sat in the hallway of the union outside Financial Aid while Alex talked the counselor into a Student Hardship Loan with which, he told the counselor, to buy his books. What he actually bought was a kilo of Maui Wowie, which he divvied up, sold, then bought books, paid off his tuition bill, *and* had money to live on for the semester — a entrepreneurial success story of growing his seed money.

This couldn't last of course. Money has a musk that attracts predation. When he talked of needing a gun, I wised up at last, and walked.

Which may have saved him jail time and a record. Shopping around for a gun had shaken him. My leaving was the last push he needed to get out. Not long after, narcs arrested his supplier and his old competition, an important bullet dodged.

Vietnam kindled at the edge of our college students' little world. It didn't lean in with the ferocity with which World War II had burst into my father's senior year, but it colored how we saw ourselves and everything we were growing into inheriting. The spring of sophomore year, Nixon invaded Cambodia and the campus went on strike: teach-ins, sit-ins, a candlelight march across campus. Every marcher sported an armband torn from black cloth.

With the white paint the organizers provided, on mine I wrote "Paix" instead of "Peace" beside the peace symbol, my little pushback against the way I was already recognizing that mass movements led to mass messages that may, or may not, reflect what you had in mind by participating.

When the ROTC Quonset Hut emerged one morning repainted, if not actually repurposed, as a day care center, the governor moved in the National Guard, many of them no older than we were. They were bivouacked in the basement of Jorgensen Auditorium and patrolling campus with live ammunition when word reached us about Kent State and the four dead in O-hi-o.

Classes and finals were canceled but no one left school, unless it was to board a bus for the march on Washington. I helped my roommate get to the bus on time and then joined a group going door-to-door in the nearby town of Willimantic, looking to engage people in a conversation about US involvement in Southeast Asia. Mostly we knocked on doors that did not open but finally the boy I'd been partnered with and I hit a house where the couple and their dinner guests had been debating the war. It was as if they had conjured us out of the heat of their own discussion. They pulled us into the living room, sat us down, and pummeled us with questions. We were all exhilarated, as if we believed our opinions could have some impact, somehow, somewhere.

The summer after my mother's death, I got myself a job teaching swimming at a day camp in the next town over. It was a job I continued with for the rest of high school and for every summer of my college years.

Swim was Brentwood Aquatic School's focus, and it's what I taught there until my final summer with them, but one of the auxiliary activities for the campers was trail riding, which meant that my favorite perk of the job was that I had permission to come and ride the camp horses during the shoulder seasons of spring and fall when the horses were not working carrying campers through the wooded trails.

I'm in the back pasture, alone with the off-duty camp horses in early spring. I have the permission of my employers to ride, but for that to be possible, I first have to catch one of the horses. I have Gill Shannon in mind.

The camp horses are savvy. As a group they watch me, watch the halter and lead rope in my hand, and they pivot away, bunching their rumps against me, closing me out, moving just enough to prevent me from getting anywhere near their head or shoulders. A buckskin, three bays, a sorrel, one faded-to-white gray. Gill Shannon's black coat is flecked with white — a blue roan they would call him out West but this is suburban Connecticut. The feathering on his legs and white splotch on his belly signal Gill Shannon's part-Clydesdale heritage.

I choose a sun-warmed rock in the midst of their grazing area and sit down. Gradually birds pick up the songs they had left off when a human entered the realm and the horses reorder into the pairs and groups of their own hierarchy, relaxing, browsing the stems nearby. Time passes, and ever so slowly I get back up, casually, watching the horses from my peripheral vision, seeming like them to concentrate on the most tempting grasses. I keep the halter close in to my own body, begin a low conversation that seeks to blend into the rhythms of their sounds, footfalls, sneezing dust from their nostrils. Moving among them, edging toward Gill Shannon, watching each twitch and ripple of muscle, each relaxed half-cock of a hoof. I am at my ease, enjoying the sun, the companionship. This too is *among horses* as surely as riding will be when I get to it. Why not savor this as well?

My brothers and I never discuss growing up with an alcoholic parent. Half a century since her death and even among ourselves, it's as if we adhere to her prohibitions about dragging out her dirty laundry. And practically speaking, each of us moved out of the family home to a different state so that we see one another infrequently and for occasions like holidays or funerals. Conversations such as that don't happen easily under such conditions. My sister and I are on easier footing with the topic. She was so young when it all unfolded, she has come to me as a source against which to test her own murky memories.

Similarly, my siblings and I never discuss the relationship, or lack thereof, each of us forged with alcohol in our own lives, so I don't know from their own lips how each would describe the path they took. From the outside looking in, it appears that one of us chose to model how one should exert self-control and responsibly incorporate drinking into a normal social life; one eschewed drinking as part of a larger decision to become part of a faith community that forbids it; and two of us made a point of avoiding an option that had already caused such pain in our lives. Now that there is so much literature about children of alcoholics, it's clear that one not uncommon outcome of being raised in the volatility and uncertainty of childhood with an alcoholic parent is to become a person who dislikes the feeling of being unmoored and out-of-control. The altered state afforded by alcohol or other drugs is profoundly uncomfortable; in today's parlance you might call it triggering, so reasonably enough, you avoid it.

When you tell time by garden bloom, you can never pretend time is standing still. The riot of lilies is passing, like the fever of first love cooling.

July

The morning mist coalesces into the windless, straight-down rain of a summer shower, seamlessly as our life dissolves into our death; it has always been there, the element in which we live, the element our lives are made of, singing suddenly in the throat of summer.

Junior year at UConn, Alex and I were back together. My rule was: if he smoked fine, but if he dropped acid, I wouldn't be there. That year he lived with the same friends he'd driven to Woodstock with in a roughly communal compound they nicknamed the O.D. Corral. Those five had the downstairs of the old farmhouse, three more friends lived upstairs. The barely renovated chicken coop housed a young philosophy professor from the university; another outbuilding, a family of Puerto Rican immigrants — the heartbreakingly beautiful parents younger even than we were, the long-lashed, black-eyed daughter and son known collectively as "Mari-tito": *Mari-tito, Mari-tito* the mother would sing to call them to dinner.

On the porch of the old farmhouse, screened by the downward-sweeping boughs of the sentinel hemlocks, Alex and I would sit on a discarded old sofa to watch storms lick lightning through the trees and flash in the nearby hayfields.

The living room of the O.D. is where I heard the broadcast of the first draft lottery. All the guys and their girlfriends crowded together around the lit hearth of that radio while in Washington, DC, an open-ended glass cylinder held 366 blue plastic balls, one for each day of the year, including February 29. The order in which they pulled your birth date out was the order in which you would be drafted for the roulette of one year combat duty in Vietnam.

We understood the war to be something young men risked their lives in to protect the interests of corporations, corporations headed by smug, overstuffed men whose own sons would never see combat. When we considered the South Vietnamese, we thought of them as trapped in the crossfire between the Communist North and Western interests. Draft age in America was eighteen; voting age twenty-one. The poster on the back of the bathroom door at the O.D. showed a startled Nixon-look-alike in a business suit sitting on the can with his pants puddled around his ankles. "If you voted for Nixon," the caption read, "you can't pee here. Your Dick is in Washington."

September 14, April 24, December 30, then Valentine's Day, October 18, my parents' anniversary September 6, October 26, my father's birthday September 7, the anniversary of Kennedy's assassination November 22, and December 6. His face a mask, Johnnie got up, went into his bedroom, slammed the door. I never did see him again.

My boyfriend's birthday came up 247th, my brother's 263th. The last third of the pool — starting at 244 — was considered safe. Mute with survivors' guilt, the high-numbered slunk away to be alone with their luck. The radio played Three Dog Night, "One Is the Loneliest Number."

They threw parties at the O.D. where the brownies had hashish and a salad bowl brimmed with pooled pills of every shape and description. I would ferry the circling toke to the next person, grab the maracas or the tambourine for the impromptu jams of "Love the One You're With" and "Suite: Judy Blue Eyes," then I'd turn in early, alone in my boyfriend's bed.

When sunlight rimmed the window shade, I'd get out of bed without waking him or the others in the room, pull on some clothes, step over the bodies in the living room, and slip out the kitchen door. Sometimes the philosophy professor would be in the shared yard, in just his ragged jeans, a shaggy Pan softly playing his flute, barefoot in the dew. We wouldn't speak as I headed up the road to the nearby farm where there was a horse I was allowed to ride.

I would curry and brush Mafair, her warm animal smell, the easy solidity with which she inhabited her own life, calmed and pulled me so. I saddled her and together we rode out into the morning of the life that would be mine.

We measure time to tame it. However much we might feel swallowed by our clocks and calendars, our invented obligations insulate us from those suspended moments when we suddenly recognize our embeddedness: the dark's cool embrace of us under that far wash of stars, or the open blue indifference of the sky, an undomesticated moment in which your feet accept the earth's unconcerned support, and the exquisite membrane of the lungs bellow the air, into and out, suspended if only for the moment in a recollection of the mortal world's conjugal caress.

Entering the final year of my undergraduate career, what comes next became a pressing question. Graduate school struck me as a kind of stopgap — a hopefully productive place to go while I tried to figure out how to become a writer. Once again advising wasn't much help. It would be decades before I even knew

Iowa or any other program like that existed. I was one of eight students out of several hundred English majors graduating that year who were chosen by the English Department faculty to take the Degree with Distinction exam, so it is not as if no one noticed I might have potential but then there wasn't the system of creative writing programs that exist now. Perhaps if I had known better questions to ask, but as it was, my official departmental adviser shepherded me toward what he knew, which is to say, academic graduate programs, and none of my other professors suggested otherwise. State University of New York at Binghamton was one of several I applied to — I remember it being described to me as a program whose star was rising.

The letter was pinned to the bulletin board at the Horse Barn at UConn. A sleepaway camp in New York State called Big Island Camp was looking for a riding instructor who could also help with a group of three just-purchased Morgan horses. I sent off an inquiry, an application letter and quickly received a reply asking to set up an interview. I had vaguely figured from the camp's name that it was likely located on Long Island, but when I looked up Windsor, New York, I discovered it was just east of SUNY-Binghamton, which had both accepted me and offered me a graduate assistantship. When I realized where this summer job was located, I began to think that the most important perk of this job might well be that it could provide me with an opportunity to ride while I was in graduate school.

It was a five-hour drive from UConn to Big Island Camp to interview for the summer job as riding instructor, so the camp owners had offered to put me up for the night. I don't remember thinking through how awkward that would be had the interview not gone well, likely because that did not turn out to be an issue.

Like Brentwood Aquatic School where I had been spending my summers, Big Island Camp was a family-run enterprise and my correspondent who had arranged my interview turned out to be the twenty-five-year-old son of the owners.

Steve had gone away to college and trained as a shop teacher and then returned to the farm and landed a job teaching at the very school he had graduated from only four years before. That might sound unimaginative but complicated reasons influenced that choice. Steve's grandparents' family had been horse dealers in Merzig, Germany, in the Saar Basin and had made their fortune selling mounts to the German army during World War I, but in the late 1930s, the fact that siblings of Steve's grandparents had died for the Fatherland in the First World War was irrelevant to the Nazis in the face of the family's Jewishness. When their home in Merzig was commandeered by the Nazis, they were allowed to move to Luxemburg, which was only about forty miles away. The

Herzes were able to bring furnishings and belongings with them almost as if the move was entirely voluntary. In Luxembourg they had a dairy farm with a milk route their brilliant cart horse knew by heart and a large porch on the front of the roadside farmhouse where Lina ran a little traveler's rest, serving farm-fresh milk and her own kuchen. But as the decade of the thirties neared its end, Isaac and Lina worried Luxembourg would not be far enough.

Isaac secured visas for themselves and their young teenaged sons early in the summer, but the family was happy in Luxembourg and the weather that year was exceptional. Only another farmer would know what it was to abandon all that they had built there and to leave a bumper crop in the fields to flee once again, but in August they crossed France and the family sailed from the port of Le Havre on September 1, 1939, the morning Poland was invaded.

They landed first in New York City but by November they had moved to the farm in Windsor, with the exception of the older son, the young man who would one day be Steve's father, because Herbert, who had been born deaf and like all of them would now need to learn English, went temporarily to a school for the deaf in White Plains. In Windsor the family established themselves as dairy farmers and supplemented income in the summers by taking in boarders from New York City, offering "fresh country air and good kosher cooking." By taking in boarders, I mean the men would sleep in the hay and Lina grabbed her few hours of sleep on the couch while all of the beds were rented out.

Steve's parents met when Greta's family came to the farm from the City for a summer vacation. The camp I was applying to for a job had grown out of that summer boarding business, the children of boarders going down the street to Herbert and Greta's to give their parents a real vacation. Gradually the informal arrangement became a full-fledged camp with camp directors from Long Island who handled recruiting.

Big Island Camp survived well beyond Big Island Farm, the dairy business having had to be given up when Steve's uncle Werner lost both arms in an accident with the hay baler. The land was divided up in adjoining parcels among the surviving grandmother (her husband Isaac having died of a sudden heart attack when Steve was still an infant); the uncle's family; and Steve's family. Werner was fitted with prostheses and supported his family dealing in cattle while Steve's family's income mostly centered on the camp. I write that so casually but imagine the determination it took to make your living as a cattle dealer with both hands and forearms replaced by prostheses.

Steve was the first of the American generation, the firstborn of the generation to thwart Hitler by surviving and thriving. As often happens in immigrant families even where the father does not have the added complication of deafness, as the oldest Steve had long been the family liaison with the outside world. All of this factored into Steve's return to Windsor after college. In addition, there was his own attachment to the land. At the time that I met him, Steve was just a few years into his career as a high school shop teacher and was looking for something about the farm to call his own. The Morgan horses were that something.

❖

Elegant as the argument of his book is I don't know that I can agree wholly with Ghosh. I don't disagree that there is a clear history of the catastrophic world-view of signs, portents, and magic having been discredited as outmoded and premodern, but at the same time, one of the most persistent stories humans tell ourselves is, *yes, it happened to her or him but it won't happen to me.* We don't dismiss the existence of what ongoing evidence of catastrophe we see — what we dismiss is the possibility that it will happen to us. Optimism that the catastrophic will skip over us personally is almost a survival instinct, isn't it?

Steve's initial plan had been to start small, shop for a young Morgan filly to raise and train and eventually breed. The "get your feet wet and start small" plan evaporated though when someone he knew among local horse enthusiasts heard about four Morgan horses who were being sold as a group: a ten-year-old breeding stallion; a twelve-year-old mare; and two offspring of that pair. The young siblings were five- and four-years-old, respectively. The brother of the pair was still entire, which is to say, a stallion, so not a very coherent group to buy as the start to a breeding operation but the four were caught in the crosshairs of a messy divorce and if he would take the lot of them as a group, Steve could acquire them all at a very alluring price.

It was an odyssey to get the four of them from Rhode Island to south-central New York State but that accomplishment was just the beginning. Only the two older horses were trained to ride. Steve absolutely didn't need, and was not equipped to house, two stallions. It was but a matter of days before the younger stallion was given to the friend who had arranged the deal. That left Steve with the odd nucleus of one stallion and two mares, only one of which could be crossed with that stallion since the other was his own daughter.

Steve hatched the plan to write to those four New England colleges with equine programs that supported Morgan breeding programs in hopes of hiring a riding instructor for the camp that summer who would also be able to work with the Morgans.

When I arrived to interview for the job, I met with both Steve and his mother Greta, then shared lunch with them and with Herbert at the Formica table in the farmhouse kitchen. The afternoon portion of my interview required me to demonstrate my riding ability on Heather, the older Morgan mare who was trained to ride, and then Steve saddled up his grade Quarter Horse mare Brett and we went for a trail ride around the river flats. The camp was located on some 100 acres or so of what had been the southernmost portion of the family dairy farm — lovely, level river flat along a loop of the west bank of the Susquehanna River. The two-lane state highway bisected the property, separating the house, camp bunks, swimming pool, and playing fields from the horse barn and riding ring across the street. Turnout pastures were behind the horse barn and rising above those was the property's steep woodlot on the eastern slope of the Susquehanna River valley's western ridge. The foothills that flank the Susquehanna River in New York State are rounded mounds between the Catskill Mountains to the east and the Poconos to the south.

I stayed that night in the bedroom of the oldest daughter, Carol. Both Carol and the youngest, Marion, were away at their respective colleges. Carol's bedroom window looked out on the maternal mound of that friendly looking woods, laced with old logging roads that now served as bridle trails for the camp horses. I remember asking myself if I thought this was a landscape I could be happy in for a summer. It seemed to me it was.

From the height of what I know now I can nearly see the shore of who I was yesterday.

I moved to Windsor weeks after completing my bachelor's degree. They had actually hired two of us for the job, me and a talented young woman from Boston who had just finished high school. Charlene and I shared the duties seamlessly, two horse-infatuated young women who had never ourselves owned a horse and thus were delighted to suddenly have care and custody of a herd of them. The camp string knew their job; I had six years of counseling experience; and then in the mid-afternoons there were the Morgans to work. Initially Charlene and I did not really understand just how embryonic Steve's plan to start a small breeding program was. The enthusiastic way the two of us presumed this was a going concern pulled Steve into our vision of things.

It was clear from the start that Steve was attracted to me but I wasn't contemplating any attachments. I was just embarking on a new phase of my life, here in upstate New York, where I knew no one. I was looking toward graduate school as my future and presumed the only thing Steve and I had in common was the horses. I believed that as soon as graduate school began that he would see who else I was and that his interest would evaporate.

But it didn't turn out that way. Come fall, I found myself wearied by my graduate classes. I wanted to write and the program at Binghamton at the time did not have that focus. It was to my mind what I termed "a professor factory," and perhaps it was just my experience but to me there was a strong odor of discontent as if many of the faculty had settled for their job at Binghamton when what they really wanted, and really believed they were destined for, was a job in New York City itself, instead of what they saw as this backwater adjunct to the City. All of this was in sharp contrast to the joy I felt to be on the farm in Windsor, among the horses, and with Steve. By Thanksgiving we were engaged, by the following May I had withdrawn from graduate school and married.

We were two-and-a-half weeks shy of having known one another for even one year the day Steve and I got married. Decades later our son would characterize this as us having gotten married "on a whim." The day our son made this comment we had just celebrated our thirty-fifth wedding anniversary, so we can be forgiven for feeling justified in having followed our instincts. We had a wedding night together at a hotel but didn't honeymoon until months later — it was spring. We had welcomed the farm's first foal that April and our wedding date coincided with when we needed to retrieve the mare and foal from the farm where she was being rebred for the next year's foal. We had mares to breed and a garden to put in — the honeymoon would need to wait until August.

That winter I was deciding to leave graduate school, I had ordered a subscription to *Organic Gardening*, and then from a small display ad in their pages bought *Gardening without Work* by Ruth Stout, a book that is still in print today. Stout's reliance on mulching became a mainstay of how I was able to raise a bountiful garden while spending most of my time in the horse barn, or with my young children.

That first summer after we married, I had the opportunity to attend a powwow held locally and there I was exposed to the Haudenosaunee method of growing the Three Sisters: corn, beans, and squash. Though French explorers mistakenly applied the word *Iroquois* to the indigenous peoples of this area, a designation that persisted for centuries, *Haudenosaunee* —people of the long houses — is the actual designation those peoples used to refer to themselves. Who better to advise me on how and what to grow in this valley than the peoples who had lived here for centuries? The interwoven simplicity of their method with vegetables reminded me of the sympatico interdependence I aimed for with the horses I was riding and training.

Using a hoe, the Haudenosaunee mark out concentric circles, then trace a furrow along those lines and plant the corn in circles, nested hoops of corn. Unlike most vegetables, corn self-pollinates by intermingling the tops of their tasseled stalks so the circular planting helps to ensure that there are no "orphaned" stalks, as happens at the end of rectangular rows. Instead, the sorority of stalks murmur together in the summer breeze and being thus well-pollinated, every ear fills out fully. In the traditional plan, beans are then interplanted among the corn so the bean vines can use the stalks for support and prickly vined squash form a border around each circle to deter the depredations of raccoons, deer, etcetera. I had been growing bush beans, which need no support, and those plants were producing so abundantly as to exceed our needs already, so I just planted the beans companionably close to the corn, a practice I have continued right up to the present. I never skip the perimeter of squash defenses — winter delicata and summer zucchini — around each circle.

❖

Filling the hours after leaving graduate school was never a problem. There were the general chores of caring for the horses; training the young stock; planning for, planting, nurturing a large organic garden, and processing the produce. I took courses at the local Cooperative Extension on canning and pond management, and at Cornell University on equine reproduction, along with reading *Organic Gardening*, *Practical Horseman*, and *The Morgan Horse*. I wrote scores of articles, principally for equine magazines, both as a way to bring in a little income and to bring visibility to our farm. And I read and wrote poetry.

An issue or two of *Writer's Digest* magazine had given me insight into how to get started in freelance writing, especially for specialty magazines in an area in which I had expertise, and soon editors at *The Morgan Horse*, our breed magazine, and at regional horse publications such as the *Horseman's Yankee Pedlar*, were pitching ideas to me, but the process whereby one went from writing poems to publishing poems, that remained a mystery to me. When I found an article in the local paper about the Poets in the Schools program then being conducted in Binghamton, famished for connection to other writers, I ignored the worry that I would look foolish for doing so and I typed out a letter, included a few poems, and addressed the envelope to Molly Peacock (the poet featured in the article) care of the *Binghamton Evening Press*.

Being a famous poet does not translate to being well known to the general public, so for readers not familiar with the poetry world, Molly Peacock has since carved out national recognition for herself both here and in Canada, though then she was just embarking on her career. The *Press* passed on the letter and Molly, bless her, contacted me and asked to come out and visit. Molly wasn't going to be someone local for me to connect with because as it turned out she was preparing to leave the area and begin graduate work at Johns Hopkins. She had the manuscript of her first book, which the editor/publisher of a boutique press there in Binghamton had already offered to publish for her, but she (and he both) hoped she would find a larger press with far more visibility to bring out her debut (which indeed she did). But that visit was so crucial for me. Molly encouraged me; she told me about *Poets & Writers* magazine, my first insight into the world of poetry publication; and she insisted I needed to call up Milton Kessler at the university and beg to be allowed to sit in on his workshop.

Clearly Milt is who I ought to have taken my poetry workshop with back when I was an officially registered graduate student. Following Molly's advice, I called Milt up, told him Molly had recommended I sit in on his graduate workshop, which he agreed to, so one semester in the mid-seventies I was a member of a workshop that met on, as I recall, Wednesday evenings for three hours. That particular semester, nearly all of the students in class were young high school teachers, several not even teachers of English, who were fulfilling their thirty hours of graduate credit to bump up the pay scale they were earning. There were perhaps three of us there who were actually poets, and I wasn't even officially enrolled, but Milt was a gifted reader and teacher and his insights, encouragement, and the structure of writing regularly for a weekly meeting were vital to me and my poetry. We focused on the work in front of us, with no consideration of Po Biz or the process of publishing and establishing oneself as a poet. Milt was born and raised in the City and was connected to the poetry world there. Perhaps he thought that knowledge and connection was something anyone would be unable to avoid picking up by osmosis. I know it was a topic I did not have the vocabulary to ask him about outright.

That one afternoon visit from Molly is the closest I ever came to having someone mentor me in creating a writing life for myself, but there was another important connection I made during my twenties that nourished my desire to write all those long decades during which I published only a little and interacted with no other writers, save that one semester with Milt Kessler. During my undergraduate career, perhaps the only contemporary woman poet I had been exposed to was Sylvia Plath. I say contemporary though she had died by suicide while I was still in high school, but that means the book of hers we read in class, the posthumously published *Ariel*, had only been out for maybe five years. Plath's poems still pack a punch today. I was floored by the poems but also made uneasy by them, the way, for instance, she could appropriate genocide, and recent genocide at that, to emphasize the dysfunction of the relationship between herself and her father. Plath's work led me to Anne Sexton, and Sexton's *The Awful Rowing toward God*. Sexton's work was electric — that book, and her *Transformations*, with its brash and feminist reimaginings of familiar fairy tales — but Sexton like Plath seems to have gained attention from the poetry establishment as much through her suicide as through her powerful work. I was looking for a role model for a life as a woman and a poet that was life-affirming, that did not end in suicide. Sexton led me to Maxine Kumin. What a revelation to me — a woman who was getting publication and recognition while writing from her New England horse farm.

I have no memory of how I got that first letter to Max. I may well have written her care of her publisher, just as I had written Molly Peacock care of the newspaper. Along with my fan letter, I included poems of my own, and was careful to include a couple that featured horses. Recipient of the Pulitzer Prize and Poet Laureate of the US (back when that post was titled Poetry Consultant to the Library of Congress), Max was widely known and admired and got plenty of fan mail with poetry tucked inside. She admitted to me later it was the poems about horses she could not persuade herself not to read. And then to respond to. A crucial lifeline for me.

Meanwhile, learning to navigate any aspect of Po Biz was a puzzle it would continue to take me many years to solve.

❖

In the wrap of summer dark, in the night pastures, you sense more than see the peaceful bulk of horse bodies near you, the amble and stroke of their hooves, the crop and snuffle of their grazing, the darkness animate, expansive, sheltered by the distant intimacy of the Milky Way's pergola of stars, the night insects chirruping, the soft whispering of muzzles in the cool grasses, the harbor of that darkness embryonic, cherishing.

August

The blueberry season winds down as summer powers on, full of the urgency of how much must be packed in, how soon the insect hum of summer days will pass. The last straggler lilies flare the flutes of their blossoms, resplendent among the emptied stalks where July's full flush had blazed. Already the autumn goldenrod is budded, ready.

At 444 miles, the Susquehanna River is the longest river on the East Coast. Though it can be formidable in springtime, because it is one of the world's oldest rivers, the Susquehanna today makes generally lackadaisical and sprawling progress from its origin in Otsego Lake, where Cooperstown, New York is located, until its outlet in the Chesapeake Bay. Our farm is situated maybe three miles north of where the river dips into Pennsylvania for the first time, before it turns north at Great Bend, Pennsylvania, to reach back into New York at Binghamton. The Susquehanna absorbs the Chenango River at Binghamton, then flows west to Waverly where the river arcs back into Pennsylvania to continue on its journey to the Chesapeake.

The village of Windsor is sited two-and-a-half miles north of our farm, just downriver from where the Oneida village of Onaquaga had been. Spellings vary. The current hamlet with that name is a few miles upriver from the main site of that original village and spells the name Oquaga.

The Oneidas were one of the nations of the Haudenosaunee Confederacy. Their settlement of Oquaga was located in the broad fertile valley of the serpentine Susquehanna at a point in the river suitable for fording, and that simultaneously provided the shortest portage between the Susquehanna and the Delaware Rivers. For these propitious reasons the spot was also at the intersection of several important trails. The wide river valley along this stretch of south-flowing river is flanked to the east and to the west by an undulating ridgeline of softly mounded foothills but at one particularly wide section of the valley there is a distinctive discrete hill known as Oquaga Mountain, which was considered sacred space and a meeting place for sachems. The river, the portage point, the trails, the sacred meeting place all contributed to Oquaga's long history as a crossroads for trade and cultural exchange.

Traditionally the nations of the Haudenosaunee Confederacy divided power between the male sachems and chiefs and the clan mothers, who had responsibility for nominating the male leaders. Decisions were made by reaching consensus between the clan mothers and the male leaders. Women raised the crops while men hunted and conducted war and diplomacy. Over the course of more than a century, European contact put those traditional ways of life among indigenous peoples under extraordinary pressures. In the wake of the multiple decimations of pandemic losses from infectious diseases for which the populations of this continent had no immunities, and the undermining of cultural supports caused by the pressures of both trade with Europeans and incursions by European settlers, the nations of the dominant Haudenosaunee Confederacy in the area we now call New York State had absorbed individuals and groups from many tribes and that was certainly representative of the Oquaga settlement. The name "Oquaga" itself is reported to be not Oneida but Mohawk (the Mohawks being the easternmost of the Confederacy nations) for "place of the wild grapes" (and wild grapes do indeed grow throughout this valley still). In 1722 Iroquoian-speaking members of the Tuscaroras who had been forced out of their homelands in the area Europeans were calling the Carolinas joined the Oquaga settlement (and were accepted as the sixth and final nation into the Haudenosaunee Confederacy, a fact that explains why the ridge I look out on across the Susquehanna River from my home is locally known as Tuscarora Mountain). In 1753 Nanticoke refugees from Virginia moved into the village and that same year the Reverend Gideon Hawley established a mission in the village, which both increased the population of Christianized Native Americans in the village and attracted other Christianized indigenous persons who migrated from elsewhere. The Treaty of Fort Stanwick in 1768 forced the Mohawks north and west of their traditional lands; many of them, especially the Christianized ones, settled just west of the treaty line in Oquaga.

In the mid-1970s, an adult learning class on local history was offered at Windsor High School, with Marge Hinman as the instructor. A well-respected local historian and longtime Windsor resident, Marge had, among other projects, been the founding president of the Old Onaquaga Historical Society, was then (and had long been) president of the Broome County Historical Society, and she was in the midst of what turned out to be thirty years devoted to creating a local history research center. I signed up for Marge's class a few years into my time here in this valley in the hopes of learning more about the history of the land where our farm is located and found at the first class meeting that two other farmers from our valley had signed on for the same reason. At the time that we took that course, Marge must have just completed *Onaquaga: Hub of the Border Wars of the American Revolution in New York State*, the book she self-published under her full name, Marjory Barnum Hinman. The book may have been self-published but it is meticulously researched and usefully thorough. Marge's book remains in the collections of libraries like Broome County

Public Library and Binghamton University and used copies seem to still be on offer from booksellers online.

In *Onaquaga: Hub of the Border Wars*, Hinman reproduces a map made in 1755 by the aforementioned Gideon Hawley, which shows Onaquaga of that time as including four towns along a ten-mile stretch of the Susquehanna River with Tuscarora settlements to the north and south and a Delaware settlement downstream. Contemporary eighteenth-century accounts reported by Hinman and others describe thousands of acres cleared for raising the Three Sisters, along with pumpkins, peas, orchards of fruit trees, and livestock. At least some of the acreage of our farm might well have been cultivated long before the arrival of any Europeans.

In addition to the disruption of absorbing the substantial population of displaced people from the variety of other tribes, Onaquaga's proximity to the boundary drawn by the Fort Stanwix treaty led to significant physical changes to the Upper Susquehanna River Basin, and increased undermining of indigenous social arrangements. The newly "opened" area east of Onaquaga was rapidly settled by Europeans, typically in the patroon pattern of landlords who took ownership of the land and the Scotch-Irish or German tenants who actually lived on and farmed the land. The tenant farmers and investors came to transform "the wilderness" into commercial agrarian land — clearing woodland to plow up into productive fields, running fences, erecting mills, introducing ferries to link the new communities to more developed markets. The newcomers to the area, indigenous refugees and European immigrants alike, sometimes in concert, often in opposition to one another, were transforming the area at a dizzying pace.

The divisions and disruptions went well beyond the economic. For indigenous peoples and the Europeans alike the borderland of the frontier presented the unmoored and world-altering space in which centuries-old cosmologies dissolved, providing both incalculable loss, and unprecedented invention and opportunity. The surviving literature of the period of colonization regularly reveals an admixture of elegy and opportunity.

In Onaquaga, denominational rivalries between the establishment Church of England (Anglican) and the New England Puritan strain of Protestantism (Congregationalist and Presbyterian) contributed to cultural disruption and multiplicity as missionaries exploited traditional tribal rivalries in attempting to advance their own version of Christianity. Mapmaker Gideon Hawley was one of a progression of more than two dozen missionaries and interpreters who came to Onaquaga between 1748 and 1777 from the Puritan John Sergeant's mission school in Stockbridge, Massachusetts. The Christianized Mohawks who made up a percentage of the town's population, on the other hand, were Anglican, and they had the support and approbation of Sir William Johnson, British Superintendent of Indian Affairs for all the northern colonies. Meanwhile, Samuel Preston, one of the contemporary sources Hinman quotes from, reported that unbeknownst to their ministers of either Christian sect, the native peoples continued with a school of their own to educate the boys and young men in traditional learning and customs.

By the time of the American Revolution, Onaquaga was a busy, multicultural settlement of some 400 people, including representatives of all six Haudenosaunee Nations, a group of Algonquin-speaking Lenapes, and even white Loyalists.

Any attempt at "truth" is partial, conditional, flawed, but if we have learned nothing else in recent years, we have learned that an honest attempt to construct such a thing still matters.

To understand what happened to Onaquaga and how the land I live on was taken from the Haudenosaunee who had lived there for so long, we need at least a little more information about the disputes and struggles that animated life in Onaquaga at the time of the American Revolution. We need, in particular, to know more about Joseph Brant.

Canajoharie today is a village located along the New York State Thruway, west of Albany, perhaps one-third of the distance between Albany and Syracuse. Even prior to European contact, Canajoharie was an important Mohawk town, situated along the Mohawk River, the "thruway" of those times. Similar to the situation in Onaquaga, in the years leading up to the American Revolution children growing up in the town of Canajoharie would regularly hear Mohawk, German, and English spoken and would be exposed to the customs of very different cultures.

The Mohawk woman Owandah was from Canajoharie. The extent of her interactions with Europeans is evident by the facts that Owandah is most often referred to in the historical record by her anglicized name, Margaret Brant; that Margaret was Christianized; and she had developed a thriving business collecting and selling ginseng for resale in Europe. Margaret comes into our conversation here because among her children were Molly Brant and Joseph Brant, two people who would figure prominently in negotiations and alliances between the Haudenosaunee and the British.

Through the ginseng trade, Margaret met Sir William Johnson. Johnson had been born in County Meath, Ireland, around 1715. Johnson's mother was descended from Norman-Irish gentry who had been in Ireland prior to the Tudor conquests of Ireland of the sixteenth and seventeenth centuries, but that one-time favored class had fallen out of favor and lost much of their holdings because of their ongoing allegiance to Catholicism. William Johnson was born into a Norman-Irish family determined to overcome the limitations of that history. William's paternal grandfather, born a MacSeáin had anglicized the family name from MacShane to Johnson, in a move to improve the family's prospects. When William Johnson left to find his fortune in the British colonies, he converted to the Church of England, thereby continuing a familial pattern of anglicization in the interests of advancement.

Johnson had arrived in the colonies as an agent of his uncle but quickly began to prosper for himself through the strong alliance he formed with the Mohawks. Johnson learned Mohawk customs and became fluent in the Mohawk language. A trader and land speculator, the trust Johnson built up among the Mohawks led to his being appointed first as British agent to the Haudenosaunee, and subsequently in 1756, as British Superintendent of Indian Affairs for all the northern colonies. The opportunities his office provided aided Johnson in becoming a wealthy man who amassed tens of thousands of acres of land.

Following the death of his first common law wife, Johnson began a common-law relationship with Margaret's daughter Molly Brant (Mohawk name Degonwadonti) who bore Johnson eight children and who lived with him for the rest of his life. A devout Anglican, Molly was the older sister of Joseph Brant (Thayendanegea), who joined the Johnson household at a young age. Sir Johnson subsequently provided the funds for an English-style education for Joseph.

By 1754, the French and Indian War, the colonial theater of the Seven Year War between the French and the British, had broken out. The inclination of the Haudenosaunee was to remain neutral. It was not their fight and they were very reluctant to risk any losses. Meanwhile, Sir Johnson was continually being pressured by the crown to persuade the Haudenosaunee to fight in support of the British. At the summer solstice of 1755, Johnson arranged a conference at his home on the Mohawk River with the Haudenosaunee chiefs and clan mothers, offering many inducements to persuade them to enter the war on the side of the British.

James Fennimore Cooper's *The Last of the Mohicans*, set in 1757, is a fictionalized account of the Battle of Lake George in the French and Indian War, a battle in which the real Johnson had an important role, and in which Joseph Brant (aged about fourteen or fifteen at the time) apparently played the role of scout for the British. The Haudenosaunee took heavy losses at the Battle of Lake George, which swung the leadership of much of the Six Nations back to a policy of neutrality.

I'm streamlining complicated times, trying to provide just the pivotal points to arrive at an understanding of what happened at Onaquaga. Fluent in English language and customs, but also fluent in at least three Haudenosaunee languages and customs (perhaps in all six), Joseph Brant was a Mohawk warrior and, like his mother and his sister, Molly, a devout Anglican who collaborated on the translation of the Anglican catechism into Mohawk. In short, Brant was a border-crosser who attracted powerful supporters and powerful enemies. Brant had formed a strong connection with Isaac, the Haudenosaunee figure at Onaquaga who was recognized as the spiritual leader of the Anglican

Christianized indigenous peoples there. At least one source reports the connection as his having married Isaac's daughter. In 1775 as the Revolution began, Joseph Brant's wife and children went to Onaquaga, while Brant himself was in Quebec, then London, then New York City. In July of 1776, Brant fought with British General Howe's forces in their attempt to retake New York; in August of that year, it is believed he was with Clinton, Cornwallis, and Percy in the Battle of Long Island.

In the months that followed that, Brant traveled from village to village trying to raise support among the Haudenosaunee to join the fight on the side of the British. Brant said he had received promises in London that if the British won, Haudenosaunee land rights would be respected, whereas if the Americans won, that would be unlikely — Brant reminded them that George Washington was a surveyor and had been a chief investor in the Ohio Company, the very land speculators whose efforts to bring white settlement to the Ohio River Valley had been causing the Confederacy so much trouble with settlers incurring on Haudenosaunee land. One of the "oppressive acts" of Parliament at the heart of American discontent was the Royal Proclamation of 1763, which forbid white settlement beyond the Appalachians. But the Grand Council of the Six Nations meeting in Albany in 1775 had already decided on a policy of neutrality, so it was a frustrated Joseph Brant who returned to Onaquaga determined to recruit a band of independent warriors.

Few Onaquaga villagers joined with him but Brant raised the British flag at the village and assembled a force of a few Mohawk and Tuscarora warriors augmented by eighty white Loyalists. The force that called itself Brant's Volunteers was predominately a white force, led from their home base at Onaquaga by the Mohawk warrior Joseph Brant.

Irma Pineda, an Isthmus Zapotec poet and writer has an essay she wrote in Spanish, an excerpt from which appeared recently on the Poetry Daily site, as translated into English by Sally Keith, editorial codirector of Poetry Daily, which reads in part: "In my mother-tongue, *Didxazá* (Zapotec), there are two words for referring to nature. One word is *nagá*, which makes reference to greenery, that which grows and reproduces, like plants, trees, flowers, maize: because there will be food, there will also be life. The other word, which we use more frequently, is *guendanabani*, which you translate as *the blessing of life* and which makes reference as much to the human life as to everything that surrounds us. According to *binnizá* (Zapotec people) understanding, there is no separation between people and nature: we are one entity."

In English, by contrast, we speak of "nature," by which we mean all that humans did not have a role in creating. At some level we know that this "nature" includes humans, but in practice we have a strong tendency to associate ourselves with our built environments, as if somehow we were clever enough to be beyond nature. This "sleight-of-mind" is related, I suspect, to our deep, unspoken desire to believe that we individually will somehow outwit that surest of characteristics in nature — mortality. Our dangerous obfuscation is paradoxically hastening not just the deaths of individuals but of species including our own. The mortality we are unwittingly inventing is not the species-renewing mortality of nature, but the dead end of human unintended consequences.

At the time of our fifth wedding anniversary, Steve's parents had decided to sell in Windsor and move into town, closer to the synagogue, to Greta's work, and friends. For some years the farm camp property had been owned by the four of us together. Steve and I had been living all of this time in the immobile mobile home he had planted on the property when he first came home from college. I was pregnant with our first child, and the breeding herd of Morgans had expanded to the point where we produced five foals that year, our sixth crop of foals and the largest group we would ever foal out in a single year as it turned out.

We did explore other options but in the end we decided to build a house and a barn on the largest parcel of his grandparents' original purchase — not the house they had lived in on the river side of the highway but the south-facing slope overlooking the lovely Susquehanna River valley, by the pond his Omi had had dug some decades earlier as a swimming hole for the summer boarders (though few of the city folk ever climbed the hill to utilize it), and which his Uncle Werner had used most recently as a stock pond, but which now had been given over to the area wildlife.

The September evening of the night before excavation was to begin on what would become the house where Stephen and I would raise our children and live the most of our lifetimes, we got into our old pickup with our then two-week-old daughter in my arms and bumped up the old hay wagon "road" just before sunset.

Stephen stepped out of the truck with a sledge and eight wooden stakes and asked, "Where do you want the house?"

I wanted the picture window of the living room of the small Cape we had planned to look out over the view down the valley, with the bulk of the hill behind us to block the worst of the winter winds. Light was already fading so as soon as he had placed the four house stakes where I indicated, hoping I was right, he said, "Alright. Where do you want the barn?"

Close enough to the house to go out and check on the mares in the middle of the night during foaling season, but far enough away to keep any flies and manure smells from the house. Angled such that the barn aisle should catch the summer breezes up the valley, but be sheltered from the winter winds to the northwest by the hillside.

The excavator and other heavy equipment were hard at work throughout the next day and, that evening, with just the scrape of the driveway-to-be and the hole for the cellar of the house-to-be cut out of what had spent generations as pastureland, we drive back up in the pickup to see how the siting looks.

On the berm of dirt around that opened earth, a fox searches. She has seen us but is in the midst of such frantic disorientation that for long moments we don't register as her most immediate threat. How hostile would the world feel to return from your ordinary day to find everything normal except for the area around the exact patch of ground that had been your home, obliterated now in some dystopian Alice-in-Wonderland of upended soil, the air crackling with the smell of the underworld exposed, no landmarks left, and the sun going down?

At last, reluctantly, the fox leaves the overturned earth that will become our home, jogs up the hill and melts into the trees. As the bird's feathered breast shapes the nest, our days of physically molding this space to us has begun.

At its best, I understand horseback riding as a preverbal, interspecies "language" that is spoken with the whole of the body, a kinetic poetry that the "poet" and the "poem" create together. Riding can provide very much the same kind of mysterious interlocking with an "other" that the poet feels with the material of poetry when inspiration is flowing. You're in cooperation with, not in control of, the writing. And just so with the horse. In writing, the symbiosis is cerebral, in riding, it is bodily.

To harmoniously achieve this kind of communication with a horse, you need to find ways to connect the signals, the aids for what you want to "say" to the horse, to the horse's existing understanding of the world. If you are trying to translate information from English to Russian, and then the same information from English to Cantonese, the processes are similar but they cannot be identical — English needs to adapt specifically to the "receptor" language in each case. Idioms need to fit within the context of native idioms.

In much the same way, training an animal works best when the trainer has adapted to the idiom of the species being trained. A good horse manager allows for the horse's sense of social order in working out pasture groupings, stall assignments, and what order to handle turnout. Access to water, shelter, and gateways needs to be planned with an understanding of the implications of pecking order. Herd makeup is absolutely indispensable to the trainer who aims to do a good job. The rider/driver/handler is endeavoring to be alpha, not the boss so much as the decision maker in a joint enterprise.

The best trainers understand that it is reasonable for an inexperienced young horse — all 1,000 pounds of him — to startle at the sudden flight of a bird or the sinuous ripple of wind in tall grasses, incongruous as that may seem to the human brain. In the mind of the horse, either the startled bird or the rippling grass can be the marker of an approaching predator, alarms that quite reasonably spark the horse to flight. We may "correct" that instinct but one does so most successfully not by force and fear, but by establishing oneself as the "alpha" of that horse's herd (even when it is only the herd of the two of you). When the trainer has become the "lead mare," a spooked horse can be finessed, appeased, and emboldened through his confidence in his leader. It is an accomplishment of profound satisfaction for the trainer, and not necessarily less so for the horse. It is a partnership you're building toward. Obedience and synergy are not the same thing, and once you've felt the latter, the former is of little interest.

I know that this capacity to be able to build partnerships across species is a benefit for me; I sense it's a benefit for the horse as well. I intuit this in the ears-up interest and anticipation the horse shows about our sessions, in the fluidity of his or her cooperation, in the bright contentment in their eye when we achieve something difficult together (my stallion, Ivanhoe, had a unique little chuff of self-satisfaction, a sound he made whenever he figured out and accomplished some new move).

Perhaps what interests the animal is the order, the intelligibility our training sessions create. Reliably safe habits are the essence of survival to a horse in the wild so it is not unreasonable that horses would also delight in the conceptual order inherent in learning a particular discipline. In our times, we may have lost faith that the role of art is to create or reveal order but it remains indisputable that art is *capable* of reproducing a sensation of meaning and order and that most human beings find that sensation pleasurable. Horses seem to share that pleasure. As we work out with an individual horse the gymnastic puzzle of their moving with us on their back with practiced grace, the horse appears to take the same pleasure in their bodies as any athlete and they seem also to derive gratification from the sensation of meaning that the training session leads to. They come to know what is expected of them, what their particular game is, and the best of them strive along with us, offering refinements we might not even have thought of, a deeply rewarding collaboration.

We present the American Revolution to schoolchildren as a struggle between American colonists and the British, as if the vast majority of the British colonists were as dedicated to the fight as Washington, Jefferson, Thomas Paine, Patrick Henry, and the other figures whose memories we build monuments to. As if the decisions as to what actions to take in the conflict were clear-cut and strongly held by pretty much everyone. Of course, the truth is far more complicated than that. In any political conflict, those who wish only not to have their everyday lives disrupted, not to lose all they have worked for in service to an ideal — or worse to the avarice of others — often equal or exceed those who are dedicated to the cause.

Among the more interesting contemporary works to give insight into that perspective of the American Revolution would be *Letters from an American Farmer* by Franco-American writer J. Hector St. John de Crèvecœur. (In our own times we have *Letters from an American*, the Substack, near-nightly newsletter from Harvard-trained historian and professor of history at Boston College, Heather Cox Richardson. Richardson's chronicling of current events in our tumultuous times, presented in historical context, has drawn tens of thousands of admiring readers, myself among them. I have to believe that the similarity between her title for her newsletters and Crèvecœur's title is no coincidence.)

The twelve letters that constitute Crèvecœur's book feature a fictional narrator, James, whose experiences resemble those of Crèvecœur himself while not mirroring them in every detail, a persona for speaking Crèvecœur's perspective on the American experiment as it was unfolding. Born in 1735 in Caen, Normandy, France, Crèvecœur was the son of the Comte and Comtesse de Crèvecœur, which is to say landowners numbered among what would be considered the "minor nobility." He was educated at the Jesuit Collège Royal de Bourbon and from there he went to England but in 1755, following the untimely death of his fiancée, the twenty-year-old Crèvecœur left England to begin anew in French Canada. He worked during the French and Indian War as a surveyor and cartographer (on the French side), but in December of 1759, he disembarked in New York from a British vessel that was carrying defeated French troops back to France, and set about, in true American fashion, reinventing himself once again. For a decade he worked surveying, trading, and traveling. He became a naturalized citizen of New York in 1765, married in 1769, and began to farm on a sizable parcel of land in what is now Orange County, New York.

The opening letters in the series were written in those years leading up to the war and are famous for their early evocation of the American Dream, the notion that America was a land of equality and opportunity where an individual's hard work and merit, coupled with "indulgent laws" that did not hobble one's ambitions based on accidents of birth, would lead to success.

The source of this freedom of opportunity in the colonies, Crèvecœur tells us through his narrator, James, is that a citizen, a man with some say over how he will be governed, is a landowner. In Letter II ("On the Situation, Feelings, and Pleasures of an American Farmer"), he points out that the ownership of land "established all our rights; on it is founded our rank, our freedom, our power as citizens," and in Letter III ("What Is an American?") lays out the whole scheme, which he believes makes America unique.

> In this great American asylum, the poor of Europe have by some means met together.... urged by a variety of motives, here they came ... by the power of transplantation, like all other plants they have taken root and flourished! Formerly they were not

numbered in any civil lists of their country, except in those of the poor; here they rank as citizens. By what invisible power hath this surprising metamorphosis been performed? By that of the laws and that of their industry. The laws, the indulgent laws, protect them as they arrive, stamping on them the symbol of adoption; they receive ample rewards for their labours; these accumulated rewards procure them lands; those lands confer on them the title of freemen, and to that title every benefit is affixed which men can possibly require.

Rights as a citizen were tied to landownership (voting rights were tied to land ownership until 1850 in the United States, and vestiges of our reverence for property rights over human rights persist to this day). What made America exceptional was that here there was enough land to go around, or at least it seemed that way to the Europeans like Crèvecœur who came to settle here. "We are the most perfect society now existing in the world," Crèvecoeur has his narrator, James, proclaim in Letter III. "Here man is free as he ought to be, nor is this pleasing equality so transitory as many others are. Many ages will not see the shores of our great lakes replenished with inland nations, nor the unknown bounds of North American entirely peopled." The perception of the vastness of the land was seen as a guarantee that the freedom can be extended to all, and that that happy circumstance extends beyond the foreseeable future.

Who is this "all" and "we" of which Crevecoeur speaks? Crèvecoeur himself has titled his Letter III, "What Is an American?," and the Letters as a whole are meant to answer to that central question.

The summer I will turn fifty-three, I've just spent the July morning, in the manner that has been usual for me for some thirty years now, working horses. "Working horses" might be an odd expression for those not involved in the enterprise. After a centuries-long interspecies partnership, in the developed world, horses have not been needed as *workers* for a century now, but for many people, even many born long after horses were, strictly speaking, *needed*, the inherent pleasures of the relationship between horse and horseman continues to exert a powerful pull and so "working horses" consists of training them to do the things their kind used to be *needed* to perform but which they now do just for the pleasure of the shared project.

This July morning, I was leading Grant, the last of four horses to be worked that day, into the barn at the end of his workout when suddenly I felt an urgent pinch at the back of my head. *Inside* the back of my head.

My immediate thought was that it felt as if a blood vessel had just burst in my brain. This is a thought you try to talk yourself out of but there was no talking myself out of the headache that immediately began to come on. The pain was like a thumb pushing steadily, relentlessly into a muscle, except this force pressed outward from inside the brain, pushed against the inside of the unyielding skull. I was starting to experience the ground as swaying, and my stomach began to feel the way it feels out on the ocean on a becalmed sailboat.

Unremitting headache and nausea usually signal migraine, but I knew this was nothing like the many migraines I had had. By this time both of our children were grown and launched on their own lives elsewhere but fortunately that morning I had a young woman helping me. I handed Grant off to Tracie and, telling her only that I didn't feel well, I went into the house to get out of the sun, lie down, assess things. I found that it didn't feel any better to get horizontal — in fact it felt a little worse, especially during the part where you were getting up or down. Unlike a migraine, it didn't help to close my eyes or get into a darkened room. I tried running my wrists under cold water to cool off and that seemed to slow the pace of acceleration slightly but as dizzy as I was, I didn't trust myself upright for long. I was slumped on the bed in the back bedroom considering my options when my husband came up the drive. Only about ten minutes had passed since that first clutch of pain. Poor Stephen was met at the door with the words, "I have to go to the hospital. I have an aneurysm that just burst in my brain."

I'll skip the details of the initial misdiagnosis: the return home, the subsequent late-night return to the hospital, the second MRI ordered by the intern now on duty. After examining the results, the young doctor came to tell me, "Lie still. I've ordered an ambulance for you," which is not something you want to hear when you're already lying in a hospital. The brain bleed had finally been identified on that second MRI and I was being sent to the area neuro-center. By the early morning hours, I was on a gurney in the emergency room of the second hospital, with Stephen hovering worriedly while we wondered why the hell they weren't getting us up to the ICU and starting my antiseizure meds like the neurosurgeon had ordered. We were also discussing who we might know that we could call at three in the morning to ask what they knew about the neurosurgeon who happened to be the on-call doctor that night. This is not how you want to choose the guy who might be doing brain surgery on you later that day.

What does it feel like to be lying on a gurney waiting for treatment, knowing you have a brain hemorrhage? I have to presume not everyone would react the same. I felt as if I were watching my brain making thoughts, watching the way you watch a loved one who is going away on a long trip from which they may never return. I felt very alone. My husband, my family, my friends were wonderful. They absolutely were. But this was *my* lonesome valley and I had to walk it for myself. I thought about what I had accomplished in my life, and what I had not yet accomplished. There is nothing like believing you're likely to die — or be vegetabilized — for revealing how you feel about what you have done with your life, and for prioritizing what you want most to do with what you hope is left of your life.

Right about the time of the early morning shift change, the intensive care unit was finally ready for me. They wheeled me up, hooked me to the monitors by multiple wires, and at last started the drugs the doctor had ordered hours before. The doctor came to see me for the first time at the start of his rounds.

Neurosurgeons are fond of statistics. I believe this is because, as trained and as skilled as they are, there remains so much we do not know and cannot fix about the brain. A crisp set of statistics demonstrates that they're keeping up in the field and that if they don't know it, it's because nobody knows it yet. The first thing my neurosurgeon told me was that 50 percent of the people who have what I had are dead before they reach the hospital (especially, I thought, if they get misdiagnosed and sent home the first time). He then broke down what happened to the remaining 50 percent — how many die after they get to the hospital, how many stroke out and never get any semblance of their life back, how many stroke out and get some semblance of their lives back — eventually; how many have aneurysms removed with good results, only to have new ones recur down the road. I remember the percentage he assigned to the group whose bleed was *not* caused by an aneurysm, who would likely heal on their own, and go back to life as it was, with a good chance of no recurrence — a tiny 7 percent he mentioned at the end — in case I was adding up the other percentages in my head and realized we'd only accounted for 93 percent with the dire predictions. The point to this terrifying little chat was that he wanted me to sign on the dotted line for a cerebral angiogram.

A cerebral angiogram is the gold standard for detecting and locating aneurysms. That was the phrase he used. The gold standard. For finding the aneurysm and determining whether or not it was operable. Just which centers of the brain . . . of my life . . . were threatened. For the procedure, a specially trained radiologist nicks into your femoral artery and threads a catheter all the way to your carotid artery and into the brain, then shoots a metallic dye — three separate shots to illuminate every small branching of the blood vessels in your brain. Naturally, your brain isn't always happy with this process. There is a risk of the procedure itself causing you to stroke, which would be why I had to hear all the hoary statistics — to make me understand that I needed this procedure, dangerous as the procedure can be. It's the mapping device, the GPS the surgeon needs to operate.

One more fun fact: migraine sufferers are more likely than average not to do well with an angiogram. The first radiologist to appear at my bedside, told me he had done the procedure hundreds of times — he told me just how many hundreds. He said he was the number two man in the area at doing this. Then he told me he knew the phone number of the number one man and wouldn't at all mind calling him.

While the number two man called the number one man, the ICU nurse sent someone to the cardiac unit to get a living will form for me to fill out. When he came back empty-handed, she got a sheet of notebook paper and a pen and started dictating to me what a living will contained. Because of the hemorrhage, I wasn't allowed to sit up in the bed but lying flat on my back, with electrodes glued to my chest, a blood pressure cuff on one arm, and an oxygen exchange monitor clipped to one finger like a spring-loaded clothespin, I struggled to legibly indicate that my husband could make decisions for me. "But don't do anything Courtney doesn't agree to," I added to my husband. Our daughter, the law school student, has a temperament closer to my own than what her father has. More patience. More tolerance for frustration, and it seemed to me we could be facing a heavy load of frustration ahead. The nurse took back the clipboard, her last task before going off shift. On her way out the door she said, "Good luck." Not "See you tomorrow," I noticed. Just "Good luck."

You're awake for a cerebral angiogram. First you get a bikini trim on the right side where the catheter inserts and they strap your head down to keep you still. Then along with the doctor and nurses, you get to watch your own brain blossom on the screen. The contrast medium, an iodine-based dye, diffuses through your brain like a hot blush. And there on the monitor are the secret rivers and tributaries of your living brain, dense and tangled as a wild rose. Beautiful, creepy, but you're too interested — both in the sense of curious and in the sense of being the one at risk — to be focused on much beyond the hunt, the meticulous search for bulges, protuberances, knots, lumps, knobs, dead-end inlets of any kind. No one around the gurney speaks of it. And what do I actually know? It's certainly the first brain I've ever seen. It's a hawthorn bush in silhouette against the snow. It's the branching delta of a river seen from a bird's-eye view. Lovely, and terrifying to think about. You need to use what you're looking at to think about what you're looking at. Every branch I see is sinuous, tapering, sleek. I begin to hope just a bit. I try to parse the energy in the room among those who do know what they've been looking at. They're professionally cheerful as they've been throughout, but there's been no quiet instant of dead air. I begin to hope. Plenty left to worry about: the hole in my femoral artery the nurse is holding compression on now, the possibility the test itself could cause stroke, the knowledge that I don't really know what I've seen. But I begin to hope.

A nonaneurismal subarachnoid hemorrhage. The neurosurgeon tells me and Stephen that indeed I am in that tiny, lucky 7 percent of people whose brain hemorrhage is a small, anomalous bleed that should gradually resolve itself, and have a good chance of never recurring. In a kind of synesthesia of happiness the room brightened, the claustrophobia of the clustered machines fell away. I'd even be willing to testify to joyful bells ringing.

Over two months' worth of birthdays I've marked by now. How many of those can I recall?

I have a dim memory of being at the dining room table in Cranston, my legs dangled airily over the edge of the chair. I'm wearing the kind of little "bubble" playsuit my mother so often dressed my sister and I in during the summer, my hair in smooth little sausage rolls of pigtails, and before me on the table is the cake my mother has made me, a ball gown of cake into which a little plastic doll has been fitted, the frosting piped into a pastel bodice and a skirt of frosting piped in ruffled tiers.

My eighth birthday, the one for which my mother indulged my unaccountable passion for horses by buying me genuine riding clothes — English-style jodhpur pants, Western-style shirt and bolero tie — and three riding lessons on the lovely palomino Sherrie. My memories of riding in Goddard Park would mark birthdays nine, ten, eleven, twelve, perhaps even thirteen.

On my fourteenth birthday, the last I would still be a Rhode Islander, my mother bought me a grownup birthstone ring. It was the summer of my first boyfriend. I wore the pale green peridot on my right hand, leading some people to ask me if Buzz and I were engaged. That is still inexplicable to me. I was fourteen, wearing a green stone on my right hand.

My fifteenth birthday, the first to be celebrated in Connecticut, I do not recall but the sixteenth was an avalanche of birthday cards, birthday wishes as unspoken condolence cards. And my first dog, the remarkable Missy.

My twenty-first birthday I was on the Cape with my college boyfriend and on that day we were in Popponesset. My Aunt Pat put a candle in a blueberry muffin left over from breakfast and sang *Happy Birthday to you* . . .

I was enormously pregnant on my twenty-eighth birthday. Our daughter entered the world three days later. Three years after his sister, our son was born the week of Thanksgiving, so that thirty-first birthday had less to mark it and has faded from memory.

Was forty the birthday we were in Connecticut at my college roommate's house where she made me that cake and paved it with every candle due? And then immortalized the moment with a photograph of me leaning over the blaze, my face comically contorted with the effort of drawing in breath enough to extinguish the conflagration? She slipped the photo into a plastic casing with a magnet backing and it held coupons and children's art to the refrigerator for years, the photo itself becoming the memory of the birthday.

Stephen saved secretly for years before my fiftieth birthday so we could at last go to Ireland as I had longed to do for so many years. Our ten days in Ireland came in July. Though I remember each day of the Ireland trip clearly, the actual fiftieth birthday is lost to me.

Years after our children had left home, married, started families of their own, we renovated our bedroom and I found the last birthday card my father ever sent me, the one for my fifty-seventh birthday. A crisp twenty-dollar bill still inside it. I must still have been deciding what to use the twenty for that I could point to as "my birthday present" six weeks later, when the Florida hospital called, urgent, what did I want to do, should they try to resuscitate my father?

Now the twenty sits atop my dresser, the dresser that was once my Dad's, to this day undecided as to what twenty-dollar item would be worthy of that bill?

At thirty, forty, even fifty, you are still yourself. You look in the mirror and recognize the image as the *you* you have become. By sixty there's no denying you're fading. Melting, weakening. Adjustments must be made. You're not the least bit open to those adjustments. My seventieth I'm reduced to near unrecognizability by Long COVID.

On early morning summer rides, every westward turn my horse Castle and I make in the ring, the low sun in the east projects before me the long slender shadow of my past self, riding the shade of Castle's aunt Bess or grandmother Kate or uncle Trep, all buried now in the meadow beyond the ring, but for now, Castle and I, and Trep and a younger me, ride together in companionable formation, my life layered and whole in the sweet compass of that rectangular space where for decades my life has been privileged to be shared with those quick and high-couraged creatures.

September

Late in the growing season the pumpkin vine erupts in a surge of creativity, a sinuous surf of broad leaves that billows over the garden fence, cresting over margins we had thought to delineate. The vine trumpets brash yellow blossoms, a silken-fleshed abundance with so little time, so little time, and yet still September sun suffuses the upturned green hearts of vegetation and the vine responds, glass-blowing bulbs of potential fruit as if urgency itself could suffice.

That evening we staked out the house site, one factor we considered was proximity to the small cluster of mature oak, maple, and hickory that were in the middle of what was otherwise just a long-fallow hayfield. Decades before, when the family dairy had still been viable, my father-in-law-to-be and his brother had used this spot to dump rocks that were impeding the machinery when they hayed these upper pastures. There's a spring that often caused a marshiness there so either they hoped to improve the drainage in that spot, or they simply already needed to avoid that area anyway. Whatever their reasoning, the rock pile meant the mower never passed over there, so in the opportunistic way of nature, acorns, hickory nuts, and maple seeds sprouted, took hold, and grew in that spot.

Nearest to the house was a semicircle of oak and maple, in the dense shade of which there was little in the way of turf. The morning sun did reach in there for an hour or two and it occurred to me that before leaf-out, there would be plenty of sun for daffodils, and that the daffs would be a welcome spring harbinger visible from my kitchen door. For most of the first two decades we lived here, that scattering of woodland daffodils and Siberian squill were the extent of my shaping of the landscape in that area. Extending out from that semicircle, another maple, a little line of three hickories, and one final maple combined with the snarl of *Rosa multiflora* at their feet to make an ungroomed but effective screen between our yard and the horse pastures beyond. The tractor, the woodpile, the toolshed all hid out behind the "volunteer" hedge of trees and feral roses.

Rosa multiflora are lovely in June when the multitudinous creamy single rose blossoms that give the species its name pump out their perfume. In June I drive down my country highway with my car windows wide open and drink in the heady scent. For all their beauty in spring, *Rosa multiflora* is an invasive species, and a reminder of the law of unintended consequences. Stephen can remember the local extension agents back in the 1950s touting the advantages to *Rosa multiflora* as a "natural fence." Vigorous growers, in no time these near-wild roses intertwine with one another to form a hedge even cattle won't mess with. Yes, a big labor investment to begin with but within just a few years, your fence repair chores are over, and as a bonus, there were the June flowers, and the bright, berry-sized rose hips all fall and winter — vitamin-rich songbird food, holiday decorations, what's not to like? European farmers have used hedgerows to fence their pastures for centuries. *Rosa multiflora* grows faster and denser at the bottom than hawthorns. Lots of farmers up and down the valley were convinced.

Perhaps it's that farmers' fields in Europe were smaller, and more zealously tended because land was in such short supply. Or that European fields were hedged with indigenous plants whereas the *Rosa multiflora* was a purposely introduced Asian import. In Stephen's memory of it, the extension agents of the day did not spend much, if any, time emphasizing that to keep the *multiflora* in check, one needed to mow regularly everywhere you didn't want the roses to take over. Whoever wrote the Wikipedia entry for *Rosa multiflora* accurately describes it as: "a scrambling shrub climbing over other plants to a height of 3–5 meters, with stout stems with recurved thorns." Three meters is just over nine feet. Let a pasture go for a season here and there because you got busy, or that field was wet that year, and you would find your pasture dotted with determined and well-armed squatters. Give them a few years to get going on hospitable soil and soon the invading bushes are as big as the tractors one uses on the hillside farms around here. It can take hours of work with a chain saw and brush hog and fire to clear the surface of just one well-established rose bush, and they spread (*scramble* is an accurate word choice) everywhere. And notice I said, clear the surface. The entire root system will now be redoubling its efforts to reestablish, requiring years of vigilance to really be sure they're gone.

Throughout the 1960s and the '70s, dairy farms up and down our valley closed down, sold out, let the pastures go. There are pastures in my valley now that look as if they could conceal at least a modest-sized Sleeping Beauty castle, choked as they are with *Rosa multiflora*.

With what level of hubris will we live on the earth? Fifty percent of the earth's landmass has been altered by a single species, us. The unmolested portions are not untouched due to any beneficence or thoughtful restraint on our part but because until now those places have been inaccessible. Global warming is changing that and you would be naive to think that nations, speculators, and investors are not already lined up to exploit what the rising temperatures are uncovering.

We are all complicit in this, few more so than an American. My farm, my garden that I love deeply, these are not a strip mall or a strip mine. The farm we husband affords space to other species and even acres that are being allowed to rewild, and yet I know my farm depends upon my job twenty internal-combustion-engine miles away. In winter, when I want fresh kale in the green smoothie I have for lunch, it will have arrived at my local grocery store from some place like Texas, the mango from Peru. Our ability to make that occasional trip to France or elsewhere is a cherished adjunct to our usual life here on the farm.

It is not that humans have no right to alter but I think of the millennium of damage done by our presumption that we humans had been granted dominion over all the earth. But must we lay claim, stake claim, claim lives? Is there no way for us to understand the brevity of our lives, feel the web that is our true home, and aim to replenish rather than to consume, to contribute rather than to claim?

I'm from that last generation to have had a brain wired in early childhood by books, magazines, still photography, who can (just) remember television entering the scene, the generation who were the guinea pigs for wiring children's brains through the flickering imagery of television and movies. First, we humans had brains wired by what was in front of us . . . then came writing, from cuneiform to calligraphy . . . information, stimulus that we had secondhand not firsthand became available to us, as did a means for storing information outside of the brain, retrievable even if we have forgotten it. Eventually Gutenberg and books, volumes of information, libraries of ideas, emotions, stimuli, centuries and nations of great minds available to us.

Alongside media for language was the development of media for images: cave paintings to sculpture, oils, photography. With television and the movies came motion, cross-cutting, channel flipping. And now, of course, the internet has expanded and accelerated what is available to us, possibly to the point of a dangerous unintelligibility. Surely to the point of a highly hazardous compartmentalization where web surfers recoil into bunkers of confirmation bias, echo chambers from which they rarely emerge.

In talking about the crap we tell ourselves, and act upon, collectively as a cultural group, I had used the phrase "blind spot" to refer to the mythologies of Pocahontas and John Smith and the Puritans on their mission from God to found a "shining city on the hill," but, of course, those powerful narratives are blind spots to some but convenient justifications for others. Memorably in the wake of 911, as the administration of George Bush Jr. campaigned to justify a war against Iraq, a state that had not been involved in the 911 attacks, then Secretary of Defense Donald Rumsfeld speaking at a Department of Defense news briefing famously said "There are known knowns; here are things we know we know. We also know there are known unknowns; that is to say we know there are some things we do not know. There are also unknown unknowns — the ones we don't know we don't know." His implication was that lurking in those unknown unknowns was the justification for the attack they were planning.

The kind of knowledge Rumsfeld did not mention in his categorizing were the things we know but plan to ignore or exploit. Sometimes the known things are known to only a few, a powerful few who ignore or suppress what they know to achieve some purpose of their own — as many suspect the Bush administration of having done to get a second chance at the war the first Bush administration had not won. Or as tobacco executives did for so many decades, at the cost of so many deaths. The reader can surely supply many recent examples.

And there are the things we know or should know but do nothing about, even in the face of mortal danger to ourselves and loved ones. Climate change and the COVID pandemic come to mind.

Why would anyone choose to ignore mortal danger? There is no single answer: because the untruth has somehow been successfully coupled with some aspect of one's identity, without which life might feel meaningless, so that the true believer in the untruth will protect the lie to the death? because we feel helpless to do anything effective? Despair has more than one face.

To pull past despair, let's look at a different way to think about knowledge, to think about the future.

In recent years, IQ tests have been scrutinized for being measures of only one kind of human intelligence. The report cards of the current generation look entirely different from the report cards of my St. Joseph School days with teachers attempting to measure and describe not just analytical intelligence but emotional intelligence and social intelligence as well.

Most of us are very comfortable believing that different people have different levels of various kinds of intelligence and that "genius" in all kinds of intelligence is highly desirable. Having lived among and worked among other-than-human animals for many decades, I don't need researchers to point out to me that animals display a wide range of intelligences, though many researchers have produced numerous such studies in recent years. Similarly, having gardened with both flowers and vegetables, also for decades, I am wholly open to expanding our ideas of what intelligence, reasoning, and communication might look like to include plants as reservoirs of wisdom about how to live successfully and sustainably on this planet.

What a delight it has been, for instance, to learn how trees protect and support family members and develop complex networks of relationship, insights first articulated by German forester, Peter Wohlleben, in his groundbreaking book *The Hidden Life of Trees: What They Feel, How They Communicate*, and since taken up and expanded by many researchers. London-based writer and technologist James Bridle writes about a range of other-than-human intelligences from artificial intelligence to plants and animals. "Cows, sheep, dogs and other animals have been shown to predict earthquakes in advance of tremors which register on seismographs. Squids and octopuses, we have learned, spread their neurons out through their bodies in ways that allow their limbs, and perhaps other faculties, to act independently of a centrally controlling mind. Spiders store information in their webs, using them as a kind of extended cognition: a mind outside the body entirely," he catalogs in an article in the *Guardian* in April 2022, just previous to the release of his book, *Ways of Being: Animals, Plants, Machines: The Search for a Planetary Intelligence*. A spider web, we might say, is a kind of arachnoid "book," knowledge stored outside of the brain, outside of the body.

Bridle describes researchers he has been working with in northern Greece who are, he reports, "farming metal." They are experimenting with three shrubs that grow in nickel-laced soil most plants would find toxic. Dubbed "hyperaccumulators, the shrubs draw the nickel out and store it in their leaves and stems where the metal can then be harvested rather than mined, all the while remediating the soil and making it suitable for other crops." Bridle tells us hyperaccumulators have been discovered for zinc, aluminum, cadmium, and other metals, including gold.

What these researchers and authors are teaching us (or many might say, reminding us) is that rather than humans being unique in their intelligence, rather than humans being the pinnacle of intelligence, there are many different kinds of intelligences from which we can, and urgently should, learn.

I was one of the mothers volunteering at my son's first-grade Halloween party, chatting with another of the mothers I knew *about* more than knew, in the way of small towns where you know people in common and hear about the lives of people your friends think you would be interested in. Our children, Samantha and Gregory, had been in preschool and kindergarten together, and now first grade. Our husbands were colleagues on the faculty at the local high school, and whereas I was a poet, Bonnie was a playwright. Bonnie was finishing up her PhD at Binghamton University, the graduate school I had left seventeen years before. It was Bonnie who told me about the new track in Creative Writing, about the program the novelist John Gardner had helped to launch there, building on the start Milt Kessler had made.

I had been journaling and writing poetry all of those seventeen years. With both children in school, I was trying to puzzle out what was next. Realizing that so many new poetry books now seemed to come from university presses, hearing that Binghamton now had a viable Creative Writing track at the graduate level, I began to think this might be my best route to making the connections and learning what was needed to move into publication. After seventeen years away, I once again applied to graduate school at SUNY-Binghamton, and was accepted. I started back to school on my thirty-ninth birthday.

❖

J. Hector St. John de Crèvecœur was not a man actively antagonist to the indigenous peoples — he shows interest in and respect for Native Americans at numerous points in *Letters from an American Farmer* — and yet it is clear he is not numbering them among the citizens to whom he refers when he describes his adopted country and refers to "we" and "all." *Letters from an American Farmer* was the first literary work to ask the question, what is an American? and the picture he presented in answer to this question was very influential. An American he tells us in Letter III is a "new man . . . who, leaving behind him all his ancient prejudices and manners, receives new ones from the new mode of life he has embraced, the new government he obeys, and the new rank he holds." More specifically, "James" defines this new man as "either an European or the descendent of an European" come to America where "individuals of all nations are melted into a new race of men."

It is clear Crèvecœur's "all nations" refers to all the nations of Europe, while interestingly he then demonstrates to the reader that "The American is a new man, who acts upon new principles [and who must therefore] entertain new ideas and form new opinions" through an anecdote intended to be good-naturedly amusing about Andrew, a relatively recent immigrant from Scotland. Clearly James believes the "honest Hebridean" has the makings of a fine American but the incident he recounts to demonstrate that, as an American, Andrew is still a work in progress is interesting for the glaring blind spot it reveals.

Having been in the colony for but a year, Andrew is working diligently for various already-established settlers to amass the money with which to buy a farm of his own. One Sunday Andrew is alone at the home of "Mr. P.R." while the family is at church when nine Native Americans, whom James knew to be particular friends of Mr. P.R. strode up, piled pelts on the porch, walked into the house, and set about getting refreshments for themselves. Andrew first tried to bar the door, then ran to get the broad sword he had brought with him from Scotland while the Native Americans ate, drank, and gave the eighteenth-century Haudenosaunee equivalent of "what's with him?" A (surely mischievous) war whoop from the Native Americans sent Andrew off at a run to the meeting house where Mr. P.R. had a good laugh and assured Andrew "my house is as safe with these people as if I was there myself."

In James's (which is to say Crèvecœur's) view, Andrew's discomfort and suspicion are some of the ancient prejudices he must relinquish while the ways of the Native Americans some of the new ideas Andrew needs to absorb in order to become an American, but the Native Americans themselves seem to be in some unclassifiable category of "people." They are a particularly colorful part of the exotica of America but they are not, according to Crèvecœur's definition, themselves Americans.

The widespread and convenient impression that the land was underpopulated (which epidemics of European diseases had done much to accomplish) was further propelled by the presumption that undeveloped land was available land — there was a consensus among Europeans that God, the Creator of all, had made the land and had urged mankind to be fruitful and multiply. This was interpreted to mean that those with the ability to exploit the land to its fullest potential had a God-given right — nay, duty — to do so. Take a look at our contemporary laws applying to resource extraction such as energy and mining if you want to see those kinds of presumptions still at work today — giant energy corporations with the means and the expertise to exploit natural resources legally have more access to those resources than anyone living on the land that holds those resources. The ability to exploit natural resources is itself a powerful permission even today (a lesson we learned in detail during the struggle over fracking for natural gas in the Marcellus Shale, which our farm is situated over).

I've brought Crèvecœur into our conversation to get more of a sense of what it was like to be an ordinary citizen of the colony in the buildup to and start of the Revolutionary War if your fondest desire was to be left alone by both sides to just go on with your peaceful life farming and raising your family. Crèvecœur addresses that exactly.

Letter XII is titled *Distresses of a Frontier Man*, the frontier, remember, being a farm in Orange County, New York. Crèvecœur points out the precariousness of the situation of isolated farmers on the frontier, abutting "the wilderness," which is a harbor for "our dreadful enemy," by which he means raiding parties that were understood to be Indians fighting on behalf of the British. "I am a lover of peace," he cries, "what must I do? I am divided between the respect I feel for the ancient connection [that is, the colony's connection to England] and the fear of innovations, with the consequences of which I am not well acquainted; as they are embraced by my own countrymen. I am conscious that I was happy before this unfortunate revolution. I feel that I am no longer so; therefore I regret the change."

Throwing his lot in with either side strikes "James" as extremely dangerous for an ordinary person such as himself. He points out what so many victims of war and rank-and-file foot soldiers have lamented: "It is for the sake of the great leaders on both sides that so much blood must be spilt; that of the people is counted as nothing. Great events are not achieved for us, though it is by us that they are principally achieved."

He has read the pamphlets and calls to action from both sides and insists it is no mere philosophical argument to a frontier man: "Must I then, in order to be called a faithful subject, coolly, and philosophically say, it is necessary for the good of Britain, that my children's brains should be dashed against the walls of the house in which they were reared; that my wife should be stabbed and scalped before my face; that I should be either murdered or captivated; or that for the greater expedition we should all be locked up and burnt to ashes as the family of the: B — — — n was?" acts carried out he says by "monsters, left to the wild impulses of the wildest nature."

Chief among those monsters in the frontier imagination was Joseph Brant.

❖

In our contemporary times there have been commentators who argue that Joseph Brant practiced restraint and compassion, particularly toward women, children, and "noncombatants" during the fierce fighting on the New York frontier, but it is difficult to parse how they are coming up with the category "noncombatant." When one is invading a farm intent on burning the house and stealing the livestock — if the man of the family runs out armed with a gun to stop you, has he become a combatant, and are you being compassionate to the wife and children if you only kill the husband and burn the house? As Crèvecœur makes clear, a stance of neutral was nigh on impossible for area settlers to maintain and the fighting on the New York frontier was vicious, and it was so on all sides. What there is no question about is that, in his own times, Brant was infamous as "Monster" Brant and blamed for atrocities, and for raids he and his Volunteers were not even involved in. Using Onaquaga as a base, Brant and his Volunteers raided settlements in New York and Pennsylvania that were understood to be siding with the revolutionaries, stealing cattle, burning houses, and killing many. In retaliation, in October 1778, while Brant and his volunteers were away from Onaquaga on a raid, a force of Continental soldiers and local New York militia, led by Colonel William Butler, on orders from General George Washington and New York Governor George Clinton, converged on the town.

I know what our valley looks like in early October, the harvest being gleaned from orchards and fields, the hardwoods blazing with autumn color, the river a silver ribbon of mist each morning. Aware of the overwhelming force converging on them, Onaquaga's inhabitants fled hastily, after which the soldiers took more than a full day to lay waste to the settlement, even though their commander, Butler, described Onaquaga as "the finest Indian town I ever saw." In their minds, Onaquaga was home base of the reviled Joseph Brant, so the American forces burned all the houses, killed the livestock, chopped down the orchards, and burned the corn crop. Though the majority of Onaquaga's residents had left ahead of the raid, more than one account from the Patriot forces reports a number of small children were found hiding in the cornfields. Several sources reported that at least one soldier who participated in the destruction left a written account eleven years later boasting that they had bayoneted the children.

The destruction of Unadilla, Oquaga, and other Haudenosaunee villages by the Americans persuaded more of the Haudenosaunee to enter the fight in support of the British, so that by the end of the war, the Haudenosaunee were considered by the Americans to be a defeated nation along with England. Native American warriors, with "Monster" Brant chief among them, had consistently been portrayed as mercenaries fighting for rum and blankets supplied by the British because to admit that the Haudenosaunee were fighting for their own land would be to admit that the native people had a right to their land, not an admission that was to be forthcoming.

Brant and the Loyalist and indigenous forces he was leading had been notorious to General Washington, particularly in their focus on destroying supplies for the Continental Army. Now at war's end, with back pay due the victorious American soldiers, the valley I now live in was one of the areas used to compensate American patriots for their contributions to the war effort. A significant portion of the land in this valley fell to Robert Harpur.

Born in Ireland of Scottish Presbyterian parents and educated at Glasgow University, Harpur taught in Ireland for seven years before moving to "the New World" where he was appointed professor of mathematics at King's College in New York City (the precursor to Columbia University). In 1774, Alexander Hamilton was one of Harpur's students. Harpur was one of only two faculty of Kings College to join the Sons of Liberty. Though not a signatory, Harpur was in attendance at the hastily gathered New York Congress that ratified the Declaration of Independence, which had just reached them from Philadelphia.

Harpur's principal service during the Revolution was administrative, in charge early on of procuring cloth from France to produce uniforms for the Continental Army, as well as trying to procure ammunition. He became chairman of the Committee for Arrangements (draft board) and was put in charge of dealing with captured Native Americans and lands acquired in the fighting, including Onaquaga. Harpur served in the New York State Legislature during pivotal years from 1777 until 1784, including a stint as Deputy Secretary of the Legislature.

The British surrendered at Yorktown October 24, 1782. In 1786, Harpur, who held the position of secretary of the Land Board, in charge of administering lands won from British and Native American "occupation," in addition to his already extensive personal land holdings, acquired two large land grants, one of those being 15,360 acres on the Susquehanna River that included the Onaquaga site.

Harpur visited his "Susquehanna Lands" in 1787 to sell squatters the land they were on to which he now held legal title. He built a log cabin for himself on lot number 122. Nearby, he built a grist mill and a lumber mill, before returning to New York City where he built a mansion on Cortlandt Street. The fifty-six-year-old Harpur married sixteen-year-old Myra Lackey on April 30, 1789, and the two began a new family at his rural Fishkill residence. Retiring from public service in 1795, after thirty-four years, Harpur gathered his family from New York City and Kingston and moved to "the Susquehanna Lands," where a new mansion was constructed to house family and domestics. Harpur then focused his energies on land sales and development, agriculture and millworks. Harpur died in 1825 at the age of ninety-three.

The village of Harpursville north of the current village of Oquaga was named for him, as was Harpur College, the precursor to Binghamton University. Harpur College is still the official name of the College of Arts and Sciences at the

State University of New York at Binghamton. The Binghamton University website today refers to Robert Harpur as "a Colonial teacher, patriot, and pioneer." In his honor, from 1965 until 1999, the university mascot was designated "the Colonials." In 1999, Binghamton became an NCAA Division I college and changed the mascot to the more neutral "Bearcats."

Robert Harpur was buried next to his wife Myra on the Susquehanna Lands; but in 1973, to allow for construction of Interstate I-88, his mansion was dismantled and the graves were relocated to Riverside Cemetery in Harpursville.

Language and narrative may be products of the human imagination but that does not make their effects imaginary. Applying their concept of the conduct of war, victorious Americans lawfully annex and distribute land the Haudenosaunee have inhabited for millennia. In our valley, Robert Harpur apparently sold much of the land assigned to him for his services to the Continental Army to those who were there farming the land but who did not yet own title to it. Harpur afforded them the opportunity to pay him and thereby procure both legal title to the farm they worked, and the rights ascribed to land ownership, most especially suffrage, the right to vote. It was not the only narrative extant in the area at the time.

Employing a different, an essentially feudal understanding of law, the land, and the rights of others, at the close of the American Revolution the patroon system, which had been in place for more than 100 years, still encumbered vast areas in the Hudson River Valley and the Catskills. Patroonships began in 1629 when the Dutch West India Company encouraged settlement in what was then "New Netherland" by selling holdings in the tens of thousands of acres to investors who then rented the land out on "perpetual" leases to tenants, who actually lived and labored on the land, and owed annual taxes on the land but who were never afforded the opportunity to purchase the farms on which they worked, often for generations, nor were they afforded the rights of land ownership, such as the right to vote. The patroon system in upstate New York endured more than fifty years after the American Revolution, until it was finally overthrown in the Anti-Tax War of 1839 to 1865.

Another narrative/force/or forceful narrative to have shaped the area of upstate New York has for centuries been New York City. We'll take a look at that through the perspective of drinking water. Securing water for New York City was/is a government project and thus, of course, the process is public record. There are a number of online sites (including the New York City government website itself) that provide details of the history: the timeline, statistics on numbers of displaced persons, and exactly which villages and how many farms were drowned to create the water supply. I will allow that my reading of those statistics has undoubtedly been colored by the perspectives I have heard from those in my own community who remember the development of several of these upstate reservoirs, particularly that of Cannonsville, the most recently built of New York City's reservoirs and the one located just some twenty miles from us. My husband and his contemporaries were in their mid- to late teens or early twenties when Cannonsville was constructed. Admittedly, memory can be complicated — remembered details can shift over time, but the emotions around an event are an aspect to memory that tends to prevail. We may misremember specifics but how we felt about the event generally endures, and the accounts related to me about the reactions of upstate communities were uniform.

To satisfy their water needs, New York City laid claim to the Croton River watershed east of the Hudson back in the nineteenth century. When demand outstripped that supply early in the twentieth century, the State gave approval to the City to acquire huge acreage in the Catskills west of the Hudson through the process of eminent domain for the purpose of constructing dams and reservoirs. Eminent domain is the process whereby the needs of the many supersede the needs of the few, and when it comes to New York, the City will ever be the many as compared with we few of upstate.

First, Esopus Creek was impounded to create the Ashokan Reservoir, necessitating the displacement of some 2,000 people. Four hamlets were drowned, eight others relocated. Next to be dammed was Schoharie Creek, which forced the removal of another 350 residents, most of those from the village of Gilboa. Having forced the residents out, Gilboa was slated to be burnt to the ground and then flooded. Several movie companies began vying for the right to film the fire but irate evicted Gilboa residents, recognizing it was being proposed that their loss and rage be co-opted, monetized, and packaged for entertainment, took back what control was available to them and torched the town themselves before this final indignity could be visited upon them.

As soon as Schoharie Reservoir was completed in 1927, the New York City Board of Water Supply (BWS) began plans to develop the Delaware River. The New York State Legislature approved plans for five more reservoirs but the BWS was promptly taken to court by the States of Pennsylvania and New Jersey in a case that rose all the way to the Supreme Court. Pennsylvania and New Jersey sought to limit the amount of water New York could take from the Delaware, and in 1931, the Supreme Court capped that amount at 440 million gallons of water a day.

New Yorkers (by which I mean residents of the State of New York — one always needs to specify that because the residents of New York City have otherwise effectively co-opted the term New Yorkers — residents of no other state have this particular reminder of how overshadowed they are in civic matters by the inhabitants of their state's largest city) — New York Staters living on the land the City had in mind to flood had no standing to protest but the States of Pennsylvania and New Jersey did have some say in just how much New York could take from the river before it reached the other states.

The Supreme Court ruling caused the BWS to scale their plans back to three new reservoirs: once again using eminent domain, the upstate New York communities of Eureka, Montela, and Lackawack were eliminated to make way for the Rondout; the ironically named hamlets of Neversink and Bittersweet were lost to the Neversink Reservoir. More than 1,500 people were forced out of their homes, farms, and businesses. World War II delayed work on the Rondout and the Neversink so after the war, the Neversink was still being constructed when work began on the largest of the City's reservoirs, the Pepacton on the East Branch of the Delaware River. The Pepacton flooded the communities of Arena, Pepacton, Shavertown, and Union Grove, displacing 974 people and adding more than 13,000 additional acres of upstate to the City's holdings.

As soon as the Pepacton was in service, the BWS proposed another reservoir on the West Branch of the Delaware. Again, Pennsylvania and New Jersey sued, and again the Supreme Court granted New York City access to additional Delaware River System water and work began on condemning ninety-four farms and five more upstate communities to make way for New York City's latest reservoir: Beerston, Cannonsville, Rock Rift, Rock Royal, and Granton. Another 941 people were given no choice but to move. And once again a drowned community was memorialized in the name of the reservoir that destroyed it. The Cannonsville Reservoir project added nearly 20,000 more acres to New York City's upstate land holdings.

Cannonsville began supplying water to New York City in 1965, not a history that feels distant to upstaters in the vicinity of these reservoirs. In 2022, Lucy Sante, a Bard professor and thus someone who had lived for a long period of time in an area near to reservoirs, published a history of the New York water supply titled *Nineteen Reservoirs: On Their Creation and the Promise of Water for New York City*, which refreshingly details not just the colossal public works project, but the toll on the towns, villages, and farms co-opted for the million-plus acres of upstate land now controlled by New York City, and the labor of the workers who actually built the reservoirs.

I can say for myself, that on my visits to the city, when I see, for instance, a worker casually "sweeping" the sidewalk in front of a Park Avenue storefront with blasts of pristine drinking water from his hose, as if such water were an element of endless supply, I see the silver water of drowned Cannonsville braiding debris into the Manhattan storm drain. I think about the oceans of such water leaking from the ancient subterrain network of infrastructure that carries the water of those nineteen reservoirs, largely through gravity alone. In their report on the Delaware Aqueduct that carries Delaware River water to the City (in the world's longest continuous tunnel), the environmental watchdog group, Riverkeeper, notes "The Rondout-West Branch Tunnel of the aqueduct . . . has been leaking about 35 million gallons of water a day for almost 20 years."

❖

Our daughter turned eleven just three days after I resumed work on my master's degree and our son turned eight a week or so before the close of that first semester I was back in school. I sometimes wonder how I got through those years as a fulltime graduate student with a teaching assistantship, while remaining involved in my children's lives, the farm, the garden, my marriage, and oh yes, my writing. I will say the housework suffered.

In the fall of 1989 when I had started back to graduate school, the English Department administration had gathered the new graduate students in the lounge to welcome and orient us. One mark of how unusual it was then to be a "nontraditional student" — that is, one with gap years between their undergraduate degrees and their graduate careers — would be that the faculty members convened this meeting with the incoming graduate students expected to seat ourselves on the rug on the lounge floor since we were all apparently imagined to be still-lithe twenty-two-year-olds. Active as I was, it was not a problem for me to sit on the floor but it was a signal as to how I had not followed expectations regarding the timeline of an academic career.

There was nothing overnight about it but graduate school did eventually give me the encouragement and the connections to begin to publish my poetry. In addition to the opportunity to take another workshop with Milt Kessler — this time with a seminar filled with serious poets — I received helpful feedback from Liz Rosenberg (including the insight that the essay might be a genre for me to consider along with the poetry). As I was reaching the point of needing to choose a dissertation director, Ruth Stone was hired at Binghamton (at the age of seventy-five).

Ruth became my dissertation director and we went on to become friends and colleagues. I would have to say Ruth was not really any help to me with navigating Po Biz — what had worked for her with getting started publishing was no longer a viable avenue in the present publishing world she told me, and she was convinced that she had no influence with "the old boys' club" that made careers. Ruth herself did, however, have influential advocates — particularly Sandra Gilbert — who made the effort to bring attention to her abundantly deserving work, and during her ten years at Binghamton Ruth won both the National Book Critics Circle Award in 1999 for *Ordinary Words* and the National Book Award in 2002 for *In the Next Galaxy*.

At that Welcome to Binghamton graduate student gathering with us arrayed on the carpet, the department chair had told us, "You have entered graduate school at exactly the right time." He believed this was so because the large group of faculty hired in the 1960s and '70s to teach the Baby Boom generation — my generation — those faculty, it was presumed, would be retiring as we completed our doctorates and the job market should be hot. Of course, in fact, in December of 1994, when I finished my degrees, the academic job market was abysmal. Those hires of the '60s and '70s were hanging onto their jobs and universities were eliminating lines of those who did retire and replacing them with disposable adjunct positions.

I spent considerable energy for years trying to find employment that would not require me to live separate from my husband, children, and the farm, adding geographic constraints to an already impossible job hunt. Meanwhile, as a faculty member put it to me with thinly veiled contempt, I did my best to "make myself indispensable" at Binghamton, working hard for very low adjunct wages, taking on administrative responsibilities as well as teaching. The students at Binghamton are truly wonderful, and since my teaching interests lined up nicely with departmental needs it wasn't very many years before I was able to teach classes that developed directly from two of my three field exams. I began directing the department's internship program and coordinating the Creative Writing Program's Readers' Series by a year after completing my degrees and continued with both of those programs for the next twenty-six years.

The Creative Writing faculty choose the readers who would be invited to the series but my duties nevertheless gave me the opportunity to connect with scores of wonderful writers over the years, particularly as I was also the faculty member of record for the Living Writers class that ran in conjunction with the series. As a state school, the honorariums we offered were modest but I would read the work of every writer who came (if a writer had written more than six or seven books, I might not have read every one but I had read several of each genre), and I required response papers from the students in the class to be certain each had read at least one, so the following day's class always featured a lively and interesting conversation. We might not have paid them much but I did my best to make sure our guests felt welcome and heard and, in that way, I had an excellent opportunity for making connections with literary people.

Ruth had retired because of her worsening eyesight. She was eighty-five but still energetic and engaged — were it not for the eye condition, I'm not sure she would have retired even at eighty-five. For the last year, I had been her ride to and from the university to meet with her classes, but as her sight deteriorated, her inability to drive isolated her too much when she was in Binghamton. The creative writing faculty had been rotating director duties, with me as the adjunct who coordinated the Readers' Series. With Ruth retired, Maria Mazziotti Gillan was hired to teach poetry but also to become the permanent Director of Creative Writing at Binghamton (in contrast to the Creative Writing Faculty rotating turns taking on those duties).

Maria, as anyone who knows her knows, is a whirlwind of energy and ideas. In short order, she found funding to start new initiatives like the Binghamton Book Awards and the Writing Life series of visits from journal and literary press editors. At the same time that Maria was initiating these new programs, her husband's health made it impossible for her to move to Binghamton full time. Wanting to hang onto this valuable new employee, the decision was made to get some reliable help for the day-to-day administration of the Creative Writing program's activities. As the person who had already been coordinating the

Readers' Series for some years, I was asked to take on the new role. With Maria's support I became full-time faculty — still contingent faculty but no longer semester-to-semester, and eventually went from three-year appointments to full time.

I had been reworking my dissertation into a manuscript and submitting to contests, which by then had become the predominant method for getting a first book out there, with tantalizing results of making it to semifinalist and finalist over and over. Finally, a suggestion from one of the writers I hosted (thank you, Bruce Bennett) led to my pulling the long poem "North American Song Line" from the manuscript and submitting it to Michael Czarnecki at Foothills Publishing, resulting in that poem being published as my first chapbook. And at last, in 2004, I got the phone call that my manuscript "Remorseless Loyalty" had been chosen from hundreds of entries as the winner of the Richard Snyder Publication Prize from Ashland Poetry Press at Ashland University in Ohio (endless thanks to the first readers who sent it on and to the final judge, Robert Phillips, who selected it). The book was subsequently nominated for the *Los Angeles Times* Book Award by David St. John. All welcome recognition. Ashland published my book-length sequence, *Appetite for the Divine* as the Editor's Choice for the Robert McGovern Publication Prize, while Ray Hammond at NYQ Books took on my third book, *Crave*.

Though I was always to remain contingent faculty, gradually the accomplishments gained me enough respect to pull my compensation up to where, coupled with work I loved, I stopped looking for jobs elsewhere. If I were paid more but couldn't maintain my life with my husband and the farm, what was gained by that?

Spoil is a human invention. In Nature — that word we misleadingly use to mean *all that is, which we have not artificed; that which has existed without us* — misleading because we have a tendency to forget to include ourselves within the confines of that definition, an omission with the pernicious effect of causing us to dangerously neglect our utter dependence on this "Nature" — in Nature there is no waste. Peach blossom attracts pollinator then falls to what we think of as ruin but for nature, its chief purpose fulfilled, the petal now adds its richness to the soil. The feral apple wizens and falls, or falls in full blush, bruising on the ground, windfall waste, but not to Nature. Browsed by deer the fruit feeds, and the seeds are carried afar, dropped to the ground wrapped in fertilizer. *Spoil, waste*, is what we say when we didn't get to use it.

Spoil exists but it's our production, the meddling, the disruption we introduce on a grand scale working from our partial knowledge, working from our ignorance. Working ourselves out of a workable planet.

❖

Why do we do so little even though we understand the consequences of our actions? Greed, despair. Here's another hypothesis.

In August of 2019, Bryan Walsh, bureau chief and environmental correspondent for *Time* magazine, wrestled with this question in a book ominously titled *End Times: A Brief Guide to the End of the World*. Just before the book's publication date he had an article in *Time* called "Why Your Brain Can't Process Climate Change" that focused on this crucial question as it engages (or fails to engage) climate change. It isn't only, Walsh points out, that the scale of climate change itself is difficult to wrap our minds around, but it is also a matter of comparatively how little importance we attach to the future, especially a future we won't personally be around for.

Walsh is careful not to just depend on what we will publicly admit to caring about. He wants to undergird his speculations with as much scientific evidence as he can collect and so he points to experiments employing functional magnetic resonance imaging (fMRI) machines. Experiments have shown that when we're lying in that metal tube, if we think about our self, the medial prefrontal cortex, or MPFC, of the brain, as Walsh puts it, "will light up like Times Square on New Year's Eve." Think about a close family member, the MPFC lights up, but less so. Think about people to whom you have no personal connection — Walsh suggests the inhabitants of the South Asian island nation of the Maldives, which is known to be at great risk of being swallowed by the ocean due to climate-change-caused sea-level rise — the MPFC lights up even less.

Most disturbing as it pertains to actions we collectively will or will not take to mitigate climate change though is what the MRI reveals about how we process the notion of our own future selves. Walsh points to a 2017 article in *Slate* by Jane McGonigal, the research director of the Institute for the Future, that revealed that the further out into the future you imagine yourself, the weaker the activation of the MPFC. In her article, McGonigal says, "Your brain acts as if your future self is someone you don't know very well and, frankly, someone you don't care about."

Surely you've already asked yourself some version of what Walsh asks: "And if we view our own selves in the future as virtual strangers, how much less do we care about the lives of generations yet to be born?"

Dying is not new but tethered to an aging body, it's new to me. How beautiful the world is when you're losing it. Past the equinox, late September offers up one last summer night: full moon in its pearly shimmer lights the ribbon of mist the river exhales, and insects sing the Edenic song of all that waits.

October

The maple in October is emotional with leaves gushing out in gold as if desire could be enough. Nightly now, we eat the dying garden down, harvest a sharp tang on the tongue.

When our children graduated from college and set out on their independent lives, one of the projects I turned to was that little grove of hardwoods between the house and the barn with its screen of feral *Rosa multiflora*. I began to envision the perennial garden I could have in place of the snarl of invasive species.

I started small with a sunny spot between the last two, wide-spaced maples. I tore out a little area of ordinary weeds the roses hadn't gotten to yet, worked in a little wall of loose-set bluestone, and planted rhizomes of the iris I had inherited from Steve's grandmother — watercolor-blue bellows of bloom Omi had said welcomed her to America the spring of 1940. They had escaped Nazi Germany the previous September, and managed to buy this farm that November. In spring, the wave of blue iris by her doorstep had made her feel at home.

So now I had daffodils in April and heirloom iris in May. And inadvertently, roses in June. Then came the bulldozer opportunity.

It wasn't the first time we had invested in bulldozer work. On our hillside farm we have exactly four level patches of ground — under the house, under the barn, under the agricultural storage unit, and the riding ring. We paid for all four. Periodically we need repair work on the long driveway, or on the pathways to the paddocks, but Steve felt strongly that what we needed to invest in now was a huge diversion ditch to collect and redirect all the water that came down off of our hill in snowmelt or heavy rains. The ditch we had built that summer swoops across the hillside above us and to the south of the barn, sending water into a natural runoff stream that pours into a sizable culvert the state Department of Transportation had already built under the road to accommodate that stream rushing to the Susquehanna on the other side of the highway; to the north of the house and the farm pond, our ditch diverts water into a smaller but similar "cut" to the Susquehanna there. Thanks to Steve's foresight and the skills of the neighbors with the family construction business who have done all of the heavy equipment work for us all the years we have been here, we have come through the multiple so-called 500-year floods the Susquehanna has suffered late in the twentieth century and early in the twenty-first with no major damage.

While we were at this ditch-making project, we decided to augment the much smaller, second-tier diversion ditch behind the house and barn that included that 1950s rock pile. The *Rosa multiflora* now choking the declivity just behind our hardwoods had to go, and be replaced with a little gravel streambed that would be dry much of the year.

Now was the time, I realized, to remove the whole of that snarl of rose bushes, even the part entangled around the trees that would need to be removed largely by hand, and to plant a perennial garden screen just ahead of the gravel path/streambed, in and among the trees.

The easy part, of course, was the bulldozer work. A bulldozer actually is equal to the task of removing a *Rosa multiflora*. But once the bulldozer was gone, Steve and I went in among the hardwoods with picks, spades, chain saw, and leather gloves. After days of this we borrowed a neighbor's garden tractor, the size and power of which fell between those of our garden tractor and our farm tractor. Some damage ensued to one of the maple trees but far less damage than our full-sized tractor would have caused, and by hand we would still be at the task. As it is, it took at least three summers of determinedly digging out roots and new sprouts before we could really claim to have won over the territory. I extended the little hand-built retaining wall of bluestone "pavers" I found in the pastures or in the woods. We made one trip with the tractor and bucket loader up into the woods to scavenge stones for my wall from a stone wall that had been built high up on the hill by one or another of the Rogers, the family who toiled here in the nineteenth century. Then we filled in the hard-won garden site with topsoil and composted horse manure, sweetened with lime. And I began to plant.

My first memory of realizing the strength of the instinct to interact with the land that is home to me is connected to the "ragweed room" I fashioned in that undeveloped lot beside my childhood home in Cranston, Rhode Island, back in the 1950s. Untended and undisturbed, what we kids referred to as "the field" was my nearest access to nature, and was a source of endless fascination to us kids.

Who but a kid would find a wide patch of ragweed attractive? I don't remember my age but I do remember the ragweed was up to my shoulders. I tromped down a square section large enough to lie down in, laying the plants over one another and stamping them in place. And then I began stripping the ragweed fruit from the plants' racemes, dripping the cushy little green balls onto the trampled plants. I spent days doing this until the space was "furnished" with the spongy little beads of the plant I could not yet name. And then for days after that, I would lie on my ragweed carpet, closed off now from anything but the swaying green curtain of my ragweed "walls," and watch the clouds animate the blue of the sky. I took such an abiding satisfaction in what I understood as this collaboration between myself and the natural world. I have never forgotten what it felt like for those days to put the field on like a second skin and watch the clouds as if they were my own thoughts at play.

And so, "my garden," as we all began to refer to the project among the hardwoods, was to me, a physical, aesthetic, and yes, spiritual endeavor. The trees were the "hardscape" of my design: the semicircular daffodil space formed the first "room"; a garden swing Steve's dad had made went into the "room" between the next two maples. I backed that space with mountain laurel while the long run to the next maple was the sunny area of the garden and got all the brightest stars: the iris, the lilies, phlox, roses, echinacea, asters.

Before the aboriginal peoples of Australia had paper or written language, let alone maps or GPSs, they had songlines. Songlines were a narrative way to map the land. The route from A to B unrolls as a threaded narrative of events that have occurred within the group at particular points within the landscape. If the landscape aligns with your songline as you walk and sing, then you're going the right way. The history of the people and the land on which they live is seen as integrated, a single story. In the Outback, your life can depend on going the right way.

In the case of my garden, the land and I stay rooted in the same spot and the stories travel by way of the stories attached to the plants brought there: Omi's iris; the Pocketful of Miracles day lily from my friend Peg; phlox from my "sight neighbor" Kit (though miles away on the opposite slope of the Susquehanna River valley, Kit's place is in a direct sight line from mine); bleeding hearts from Joelle; brunnera and lily of the valley from Marsha; and the many, many plants Louise has enabled me to select. The mountain laurel I chose to remind myself of my high school and college years in Connecticut; the hostas I planted so I would have greenery to wind into my daughter's bridal bouquet; the bronze mums that lined the garden "aisle" for my son's wedding came back for many years. Crocus to trout lilies to spring beauties, daffodils and forsythia, bluets, violets, mountain laurel, peonies, lily-of-the-valley to false indigo, catmint, roses, Asiatic lilies, phlox, echinacea, day lilies, to asters and chrysanthemums — a calendar of blossoms that are a mix of purchases, gifts, transplants, and wild volunteers. The garden is calendar, history, songline, an intricate connection.

How can anything about the past — my past, anyone's past, everyone's past — matter in the face of the Amazon burning? In the face of all the Amazons of Earth's history burning?

How does a rain forest, a region drenched with hundreds of inches of rain each year, burn? You need to cut the trees down on purpose, let them lie for a few months to dry out and then deliberately light them on fire. Burn a large enough area and drought will set in, making the next blaze easier to produce.

The fires in the Amazon are being set to clear the land for cattle grazing and soy production.

The myopia of Brazil's arsonists is metonymy for the wider, longer burning: the 260-million-year-old coral reef buried beneath West Texas that we pump to the surface, the 300-million-year-old dormant jungles beneath West Virginia and the north of England, the ancient sea beneath Saudi Arabia, reservoirs of the rare oxygen our planet wears as a shawl, the vapor of life. Even as my fingers hover over the keyboard, the pulse of electricity that powers the screen, that lights the room, the tank of gasoline that motors me to work, to the grocery store, prehistoric forests in flames, consumed, turned to carbon, turning what nurtures us to waste.

Early in the new millennium, Bonnie Culver, the same Bonnie I'd chatted with at the elementary school Halloween party back in the late 1980s and thus been inspired to go back to graduate school, asked if I'd be interested to be involved in a focus group for a new idea she had the support of her university for exploring. Bonnie had completed her PhD at Binghamton a few years prior to me and had managed to snag a tenure-track position at Wilkes University in Wilkes-Barre, PA, over an hour away but arguably a commuting distance position from our hometown. By the early aughts, Bonnie was tenured, had moved to Wilkes-Barre, and had spent time as a dean of the university. She had persuaded her colleague Mike Lennon that it would be a grand idea for the two of them to found a low-residency graduate creative writing program with a heavy reliance on online delivery. I was fortunate enough to be invited in at the ground floor and thus began a rewarding experience of interaction with an exceptional cast of creative minds in five genres. The low-residency model meant we were together twice a year for an intense residency week, with a six-month break between residencies. It was enormously inspirational and nurturing to have those twice-a-year faculty readings — open readings with students, alum, and community members but also among your fellow faculty — perceptive friends for whom you could try out material you were working on — unlike anything I had ever had in my writing life before. The program has grown and morphed over the years but it is still a source of support and inspiration that I value.

Season of mists and mellow fruitfulness. It's been two hundred years now since Keats wrote of autumn's overflow and its clammy cells. On the coast of British Columbia north of Vancouver, an emaciated mother grizzly and her two cubs have been photographed on Vancouver Island. One month before hibernation they are gaunt as bears emerging from a winter den, no bulk of bear where the winter stores of her body should be. She's a refugee, having used more of her already depleted reserves to swim with her cubs to Vancouver Island (where grizzlies are not native) in search of food. A report published by *Fisheries and Oceans Canada* (and elsewhere) points out that Canada's climate is warming twice as fast as the global average, and Canadian authorities warn that warming sea waters and the diseases spread by commercial fish farms, have devastated the stocks of wild salmon, leaving fishermen short, and the bears starving.

Farther north in Alaska's Katmai National Park, the bears are gorging and the park is celebrating Fat Bear Week. The disparity, too, is a harbinger of our future.

Meanwhile at a similar latitude, Siberia is also experiencing the more rapid warming Canada reports, and there, the very ground is shifting beneath millions as the ancient layer of ice and frozen dirt called permafrost has lost its permanence and is thawing. The sludge of thawing permafrost turns agricultural land, and the land on which villages and cities have been built, into swamps, lakes, burbling bubbles of no-man's land. Already half of the region's arable land has been lost. Not will be lost, has already been lost. Have I mentioned the smell? Permafrost preserves, it prevents decay. Plants and animals that died millennia ago are exposed now and decomposing, releasing gases, particularly carbon dioxide, that accelerate the already speeded-up climate change.

Instinct sparks an immediate and full-throated response to threats that are apparent and impending — the swerving car, the bear in the wood on our hike, the explosion — but the lulling sense of the innocuous that pervades nearly invisible menaces are a large part of why those can be the deadliest of risks. The little skin of water in the saucer beneath the large pot of geraniums by the back door is pool enough for the mosquito to cradle her egg that hatches out into a wriggler, a larva that mutates to pupa, or tumbler, from which emerges the adult mosquito, the females of which set out on a quest for a blood meal. Should she feed on a bird infected with West Nile — some 250 bird species can contract the virus, with the loquacious corvids (crows, blue jays, and ravens) and balletic raptors (hawks, eagles, and turkey vultures) being the most vulnerable — if the mosquito feeds on you next, say as you serenely watch the August sunset from your back patio, that maddeningly itchy, tiny eruption on your forearm could potentially lead to headache, high fever, neck stiffness, muscle weakness, stupor, disorientation, tremors, seizures, paralysis, and coma. Even death. The percentage is not high, but modern medicine can do no more than support the body in its fight. We have no treatment to combat West Nile itself.

Or consider that miniscule speck of an insect the black-legged deer tick, potential carrier of inchoate miseries in myriad forms: Lyme disease, but also anaplasmosis, babesiosis, Borrelia mayonii and miyamotoi, and Powassan disease. And that's just the deer tick. The dog tick, Lone Star tick, Rocky Mountain wood tick have their own areas of specialization.

Is it necessary to mention the unseen, airborne SARS-CoV-2 coronavirus that has brought the world COVID-19 — currently the most brutish of thousands of viruses out there? Besides these threats to individuals looms the collective calamity of climate change, incremental, normalized, capable of being rendered nearly invisible, leaving us comfortable in our procrastination.

What word will we need to invent for immigration when it is the country, the home, the planet that is leaving the people behind . . . forced migration from which there will be no return . . . all the immigrants in the situation of my grandfather who never saw home again . . . when home at last migrates, leaves us behind as a consequence of our mistreatments . . . how hollow . . . how cold the word we invent will need to be.

And in the area of crap we forget to tell ourselves, crap that really matters that we're ignoring: your tax dollar and mine are still going to subsidize the fossil fuel industry. Yes, subsidize. We're paying to enrich the people promoting the most destructive thing humans do on a regular basis: pumping sequestered carbon out of the earth and burning it out into the atmosphere. This benefits no one on the planet. Apparently fuel company executives and employees, and their lobbyists, believe it benefits them monetarily in the short run, but when we look at the damage the planet is sustaining, this benefits no one. And yet it continues. Not only are we *not* reducing, we're paying to encourage them.

❖

I wasted no time contracting COVID-19. Early in March of 2020, the week before the World Health Organization declared COVID to be a pandemic, the students at Binghamton University had all gone home for a brief late-winter break. We were aware there was a health threat out there in the world, much as we had been aware in recent years of the epidemic threats of Ebola, SARS, swine flu, and Zika, but being American, we presumed our government, as it had done with those previous threats, was monitoring and using science to protect us. And would keep us informed. If we should be on alert, we presumed, we would have been told so.

In a readiness move, on the eve of students returning to class from that winter break, the university sent a call out on the faculty listserv for twenty professors willing to be a test group shifting to online delivery of their course materials. This was presented as an "abundance of caution" contingency plan in case this coronavirus did escalate in the US. Lining up to switch to online sounded like a prudent idea to me, especially since I had years of past experience delivering my

Contemporary American Poetry class in an online format through the Blackboard app, so I immediately volunteered to be in that pioneer group.

We gathered for ordinary in-person classes and office hours that next day. At the time the COVID cases in the US the public knew about were among people who had traveled abroad, especially in China, and the very first few "local transmission" cases reported were all on the West Coast. American travelers overseas were alerted and looking to get home before the situation worsened, but that early on, COVID-19 was a news story in the background for almost all Americans.

At Binghamton University, typically some 60 percent of the student body comes from the New York metropolitan area, and looking back on the return to classes from the vantage point of even a couple weeks later, we were realizing that meant the streets, subways, elevators, cafés, etcetera that that huge percentage of our students had just returned from had every likelihood of having brought them in contact with many of the overseas travelers flooding into the US through New York, as they raced ahead of looming travel bans — travelers who poured in unscreened, uninformed.

That one, in-person day back, I let my students know we would be transitioning to asynchronous online delivery effective immediately and spent a couple of hours in my small windowless office with my work-study student, a lovely young woman just returned from New York City, accomplishing administrative work for the Readers' Series and the Internship Program (all of which would ultimately have to be undone/redone). Rather than feeling foreboding or anxiety, I calmly felt as if I were taking more precautions than most.

Already snugly at home that early in March of 2020, I was unworried and unaware during the days the virus incubated within me. Until the morning I awoke at three a.m. with stomach pain, chills, and then sweating, trembling.

"It can't be COVID," the miniaturized televisit doctor told me from my iPhone. "That's a respiratory disease and you have no fever, no cough, no difficulty breathing. Rest, stay hydrated, don't go near the hospital unless you can't breathe."

Of course, the doctor's pronouncement that "it could not be COVID" was a mark of how much all of us didn't know that early on. I lay in bed that day one of what we eventually understood to have been COVID with a fatigue so profound I could think of rolling over or shifting an arm but I could not find the energy to accomplish it. No strength, no appetite, indeterminate aches.

As short on available tests as the country was back then, no one considered wasting a precious test on someone who was breathing fine, and by the time enough new information accumulated such that my primary care physician was finally willing to allow that I might have an atypical case, it was too late for the test to be reliable. So, one was never administered.

Around two weeks in, it seemed to me I was improving. The acute phase of COVID for me did not feel mild but I would be willing to characterize it as moderate. And then the Long COVID set in around dinnertime on a Tuesday evening.

Long COVID walloped me with renewed fatigue, brain fog, and a breakdown of systems from digestive to nervous to immune so profound that there was nothing in the sarcophagus of my misery but stasis, and fear. Not fear of dying so much as consternation sparked by the feeling already in place that the "me" I was is gone, evaporated in a way that makes the sense I ever had of having a self feel illusionary. I know all the postmodernist theorizing about the concept of self always being illusionary, polysemous, about the language speaking us, but when the everyday sensation of self we use to navigate ordinary life estranges from us, the destabilizing vulnerability of that is not interesting but terrifying.

Along with the feeling of evaporated identity was the realization of how alone I was. For all the medical establishment could do for me in early spring of 2020, I might as well be far out on the prairie in a nineteenth-century sod hut. You will die. Or you won't. There's no research to be done, specialists to visit, options to choose among. Stay home, stay hydrated.

One thing that distinguishes COVID-19, and in particular Long COVID, is the vast and shifting menu of symptoms you might succumb to. One sufferer in an article I read referred to COVID as "an advent calendar of symptoms" — various and seemingly a new one every day. In addition to the stomach pain, the lack of appetite, the fluctuation between shivering and sweating, my most prominent and persistent symptoms were exhaustion paired with electrification — the nervous system too revved to lie still, let alone sleep.

Long COVID, especially in someone without test results, was a no-man's land. At first my primary was sympathetic on our telemedicine calls but patience wore out. As the exhaustion, brain fog, neuropathy, insomnia, weight loss, nightmares dragged on, she began suggesting tranquillizers for my anxiety. I kept insisting I wasn't having symptoms because I was anxious; rather, I was anxious because of my symptoms. The gaslighting on top of the debilitation was frightening and isolating, especially on those occasions when my husband's faith wavered. How alluring it was to believe it was all in my head, that there could be a pill to give us our lives back.

The Colorado River is "overallocated," bureaucratic-speak for more water is being used than what is being replenished. This has long been true. "What has been a slow-motion train wreck for 20 years is accelerating, and the moment of reckoning is near," John Entsminger, general manager of the Southern Nevada Water Authority, which supplies the Las Vegas area, is quoted as saying in an article in the *Los Angeles Times* — Los Angeles, Las Vegas, and Denver all being part of the nearly 40 million people in the American Southwest who depend for their water on the Colorado River.

Those cities are only a piece of the problem. Traveling in Utah to see Zion and Bryce Canyons, we spent a night at Tropic, Utah, passing bright circles of lush green alfalfa, artificially bright against the red rock dust of the ground around those surprising polka dots of emerald. We asked the wranglers at the trail ride we went on the next day at Bryce about hay for their remuda of horses and mules and they confirmed hay in their area was alfalfa grown in precise circles scribed by the irrigation system. In fact, 80 percent of Colorado River water goes for agriculture, a large portion of that to feed cattle that go to America's steak houses, Burger Kings, and supermarkets, as well as abroad, an intricate, profitable system that is speeding up the "aridification" of the Southwest, "aridification" being apparently a new, gentler way of saying "desertification." It's an unsustainable system but the system is so large that it is like the snake with its own tail in its mouth that seems incapable of recognizing that it is consuming itself. How can we collectively stand back far enough to view the whole picture and slow down our own self-destruction?

Somewhere in the dark nights of pacing, when I could not sleep, could not even lie still, I came to recognize COVID would not kill me now. It has already shortened my life, I was sure. It will rearrange what time I have left. But I'm not going to be one of those who goes from "we thought she was getting better" to "she's on a respirator." About the time I was deciding this, pacing from bedroom to study, study to bedroom as dawn leaked into the darkness, I found myself thinking, "This is the day the Lord has made; let us rejoice and be glad in it."

Having spent those elementary school years at a parochial school, many a memorized prayer floats back there in the memory vaults. When I gave it any thought, I had always presumed that verse from the Psalms was some kind of sunny, happy-days-are-here-to-stay greeting, but now with surprise I recognize the words are instead hard-won and born of pain. "This is not what I expected, not what I hoped for," the psalmist was saying all those thousands of years ago, "but the one choice I do have some control over is to find some way to be glad in what day has been given to me." The realization fell somewhere between a balm and a bitter pill to swallow.

My doctor and I agreed the one therapeutic available to me is to support my immune system — give it the best shot I can to pull me through and so I develop a ritual of support: in bed by ten at night until six or seven in the morning, except when I cannot lie still. Sometimes after pacing, enough tension has been released in the neck and back that I fall back asleep, cocooned in the soft blanket with the encouraging mottos — *courage, peace, energy, hope, resilience* — sent by a friend. Come morning, get up. Drag yourself about. You need to force yourself to eat, being rigorous about the value of what you eat. Pacing again as you eat, a spoonful at a time. Does the movement help to settle the stomach or just provide distraction? Shuffling room to room at the pace of a dirge, you can feel how the sight of you frightens your husband, but there is no energy to alter anything on that account.

Back in that other lifetime of early March, I had started seeds for the large organic garden we always plant. Examining the flats for signs of growth is my morning prayer. Each day I pull myself outside, slog about in the sunshine using my phone to photograph the crocuses, andromeda, the forsythia, the spring beauties, trout lilies, ice out on the farm pond, daffodils, tulips, lilacs, and crab apples. Post the pictures to Facebook, text them to friends. Trying to feel purposeful. Connected. Alive.

Stephen is spending hours readying the garden for planting. It's a positive activity, he's close by if I need him but he can spend a few hours not looking at me with my hollowed-out eyes and slumped shoulders. Near Memorial Day, the started plants are hardened off, seeds ready to go in. I do what I can to help, treasuring the sunshine, the normality, the feeling of accomplishing something but often find myself roundly punished for my efforts. Put in a row or two of peas or beans, go in and sit down. Exertion sends the nervous system into a tailspin of vertigo, nausea, profound exhaustion. Hours of feeling battered because you dared to do that much. We're used to healing as a progressive process, gradually improving each day. With COVID there are what seem to be endless "false springs," and then "winter" slaps you back down.

By late May I shade the truth to get the antibody test — my primary care's assistant says I need to be two weeks past symptoms for the antibody test, but it doesn't look to me like "no symptoms" is a stage I'm likely to see. My issues have taken on a different quality though. The neuropathy is dissipating, for instance. I am still weak and often dizzy but I can now brush my teeth without having to grip the counter to steady myself and keep upright. And the terrifying nightmares where you feel inhabited, attacked. Those spells that make it hard to hold onto any sense of purpose, to remember why it is supposed to be important to push on. Haven't had one of those in a while.

I want the antibody test in no small part because if I could test positive, that would get my doctor back on board with what I am experiencing. She still would not know how to help me but at least she would not be working against me. But the test comes up empty. Not detected.

The doctor and I come to a détente where we agree on a treatment plan though she believes us to be treating anxiety and I believe us to be treating Long COVID. She wants me on Pepcid and tranquillizers. I'm good with the Pepcid — studies out of China have shown that to be the right choice for digestive symptoms from COVID. I've already begun using a meditation app and lavender essential oils to reduce the anxiety and tension, anything that has the possibility of boosting the serotonin. In the hopes of alleviating the insomnia, in place of the Trazadone my doctor has prescribed, I want to try melatonin and CBD. The doctor agrees it's reasonable for me to try my plan for a couple of months. My plan for the rest is to resume seeing my chiropractor and to begin acupuncture.

My chiropractor is someone I have been seeing as needed for close to twenty years. He finds two pinched nerves, one in the neck, one in the back, likely caused by a combination of the tension and the jury-rigged slope of pillows I've been attempting to sleep on as a means to counteract the pooling of congestion in my head when I lie down, a side effect of both seasonal allergies and the inflammation going on in my body. The adjustments bring some degree of relief to both the tension in the neck and back, and some of the stomach troubles as pain-induced acid flow reduces. Plenty of jaw, neck, overall body tension remains and we set up a series of weekly visits. Dr. L. makes me aware of the barometer of the tongue: how a tongue flattened against the roof of the mouth is just a step from a clenched jaw or grinding teeth. The tongue needs to rest easy in the groove of the lower jaw, tip against the lower teeth. Consciously stretching, loosening, settling it there we hope can help build the muscle memory for it to be there on its own. Reminding the tongue to rest and the jaw, neck, back, and shoulder muscles to relax feels like a full-time job.

Those of us convinced of the climate catastrophe have shifted to thinking of our photographs and poems as somehow less ephemeral than the landscapes, animals, and weather conditions we scramble to elegize.

After weeks of conflagration on an apocalyptic scale, the benediction of the rains comes slashing down on Australia whipped by hurricane force winds

October trees spend their emotion in exuberant abundance of gold that pools around their trunks while overhead chevrons of geese row the sky's crisp azure, holding in view the Susquehanna River's silver sinew, which will chart their way to winter haven.

November

Milky sun lights the shards of soft snow filtering to us like a whispered warning from a crueler future. Come morning a scattering of snow has sugar-shingled patches of roof and tufted the lawn to worsted wool in dawn's gray light.

National history is personal history, national identity, personal identity. The events — political, cultural, epidemiological, and climatic — which metastasized tumorously around the year 2020 bring that truth into sharp focus. Also, the truth that the human imagination, particularly as manifest in those cleverest of inventions, language and narrative — continue to shape and steer what we do to one another and to the planet in ways that outrun our control, our imaginings. Shakespeare might observe that we hoist ourselves on our own petard. With the implacable serenity of stone, climate change and pandemic will leave us to die of our own false narratives. Repetitions of falsehoods seem eventually to persuade the agile but limited human mind, but *what is* remains impervious.

What is will ultimately run us through with the fictional swords we have forged, those imaginary narratives of unearned optimism about the triumph of technology and our own cleverness — or alternatively, about a deity that is looking out for us and therefore we need do nothing — those frail tales wielded against climate change and pandemic.

Years before COVID had emerged anywhere in the world, I had had a conversation with a friend, a pediatric dentist, who had told me about a mysterious condition that had struck her postpartum, leaving her unable to walk. Not only was she unable to work but her mother had had to move in with them to care for the baby. The specialists were stumped. Finally, in desperation my friend had tried acupuncture. If you ever have a problem Western medicine can't solve, she had told me . . .

Dr. W. had been raised in China, trained by her father and her grandfather. She is the seventh generation in her family to be an acupuncturist. On that first visit, Dr. W. looked at my palms, at the soles of my feet, and had me drop my mask for a moment to show her my tongue. With each examination she shook her head sadly, murmuring, *Oh no, oh no.*

Eventually I learned that what worried her was not just that her exam showed a virus having ravaged my nervous system — which virus didn't seem to interest her much — but also that I had an unusually sensitive nervous system. This was not going to be a quick or an easy fix. But she was confident she could help me. The havoc of imbalance COVID had created was exactly the kind of condition acupuncture seems most poised to improve.

My friend who had given me that blanket with the encouraging phrases is a nurse who had worked for years in a cardiac practice. At that practice, she told me, someone with your symptoms would be diagnosed with dysautonomia. I google *dysautonomia* — a disturbance of the autonomic (which is to say the unconscious) nervous system and agree with her completely — yes, those symptoms describe me. Two days later I read one of the early articles on the beginnings of research into Long Haul COVID and one of the first things they say is that sufferers' symptoms are like those of patients with dysautonomia. Unfortunately, medical science doesn't really know how to help patients with that syndrome either but this begins to give vocabulary to what I am experiencing. And I'm pleased to read that some doctors recommend acupuncture as a way to help people with dysautonomia.

I am caught somewhere between hope that I might someday wholly return to the life I spent my adult years building, and a psychic region that fluctuates between despair, and resignation that I must find a way to build something of what remains of my life from the shards I have left.

It's a fool's errand to try to chart progress with Long COVID day-by-day or even week-by-week, but I found if I went back two months' time, I could see improvements. June was better than April, August better than June. As a writer it was devastating that now months after my symptoms had begun, I could not seem to even think about writing, and in a phenomenon I had never experienced, I could not concentrate enough even to read. Finally, it occurred to me to try an audio version of a lighter read, something focused on plot that could lead my mind by the hand. That was helpful. And I began to sing. To play upbeat music I could sing along with. Anything to raise the feel-good hormones.

In my old life, summertimes I would work five horses in a day. Now if Stephen helped me get the horse ready, some days I felt well enough that I could poke around on Castle, first just at a walk, then walk and a bit of trot. The day I rode him in the ring for fifteen to twenty minutes and then rode out into the upper pasture was glorious — a first flush of at least momentarily feeling myself. Puttering in the garden and a walk on the farm continue to be my daily shot of serotonin and now add in a few sessions a week working with one horse. Despite the lack of a regular workout, Castle continues to be angelic, as if he could somehow intuit how much I needed him.

The weekly chiropractic appointments and biweekly acupuncture sessions remain my lifeline, those two doctors' steady confidence that they can get me better perhaps as important as the treatment itself.

❖

Yes, language can construct narratives that blind us to *what is* instead of revealing *what is*, and this construction of obfuscating narratives can be inadvertent or intentional (or some mash-up of both). The power of controlling the narrative, the power of policing the definitions, can be world-altering both for those with the power, and most of all for those subject to that power. Now and then though the target of some intentional language distortion or another actually finds a way to seize the power and reverse the dynamic.

One small example of the struggle to harness our clever but slippery invention, language, to the truth-telling we (I should probably say, *many of us* rather than *we*) hope for from it: sleek, kinky, flowing, nappy, silken, coarse are all adjectives one can use to describe various types of hair. The words' denotations delineate specific physical characteristics of the hair type. But as we well know, these are not neutral words when applied to hair. Each of these adjectives carries with it long-held connotations that cannot easily be shaken off. The descriptors are colored with preconceptions of good or bad, desirable and undesirable.

The Afro-Caribbean-Canadian poet Marlene NourbeSe Philip has a poem in her 1969 collection *She Tries Her Tongue, Her Silence Softly Breaks* that demonstrates how resistance to such limitations can work. The poem, called "Meditations on the Declension of Beauty by the Girl with the Flying Cheekbones," hammers apart conventional syntax to ask

> If not in yours
> In whose
> In whose language
> Am I
> If not in yours
> Beautiful

Which highlights the challenge of bending a language to tasks it has been designed to fail at. NourbeSe Philip rises to the challenge of her own question within the poem, describing the

> Girl with the flying cheekbones:
> She is
> I am
> Woman with the behind that drives men mad

and the man

> Is the man with the full-moon lips
> Carrying the midnight of colour
> Split by the stars — a smile

But of course, it takes many such successes to overcome centuries of negative associations.

In American English the most irradiated of words and the most visible of campaigns to claim control over definition by the people being defined by that word would surely be the *n*-word, but there are plenty of other examples. *Powwow* is Algonquin for a social gathering with sacred implications. It is one of the Algonquin words absorbed into English where it kept the denotation of a gathering but acquired a connotation of triviality — one powwows over what to have for dinner but summits about world peace. But native tribes have resisted this co-option and claimed authority over denotation and connotation of their own term, holding impressive powwows as important celebrations that preserve and extend their culture, social gatherings of great richness. This summer during the week I was fortunate enough to spend in Mashpee, the Wampanoag Tribe held their Annual Powwow at the traditional Powwow Grounds next to the tribe's gleamingly modern Community and Government Center. All three days of the event Great Neck Road was lined for miles with the vehicles of attendees and visitors.

At the same time, under the United States's first indigenous person Secretary of the Interior, Deb Haaland, the Algonquin word *squaw* has formally been declared derogatory and Secretary Haaland has ordered a task force to find replacement names for valleys, lakes, creeks and other sites on federal lands that use the word. Denotatively the word simply means "woman" but the Interior Department statement points out that connotatively "The term has historically been used as an offensive ethnic, racial, and sexist slur, particularly for Indigenous women." The world-famous California ski resort, S____ Valley, site of the 1960 Winter Olympics, had already changed its name to Palisades Tahoe and now federally held sites will be following suit.

Though my experience of COVID has involved no respiratory symptoms, I have a pulmonologist I see annually for another condition. My sarcoidosis has been in remission for some time but given all that has gone on in 2020, I am eager as my November annual examination rolls around to make sure the condition is still in remission, and I also want to hear what Dr. M., a pulmonologist who has had to be dealing with more typical COVID cases since spring, has to say about me.

Her first concern is to make sure the sarcoid has not revived under the pressure of the virus this spring. Lungs sound good. She wants to draw blood to confirm the sarcoid is still in remission but she agrees it certainly sounds to her like I had COVID and am now dealing with Long COVID.

"Why didn't it show up on the antibody test?" I ask.

"Exactly what I would have expected," she replies. "The immune system is complicated and especially with the sarcoidosis you fought off some years ago, I would expect T cells to have been your first line of defense with COVID."

"Why didn't my husband catch it?"

"I suspect because your symptoms were not respiratory."

I go through my whole scheme for recovery. To my relief, Dr. M. endorses everything I am doing. No one really knows what to do but based on what little is known so far, my pulmonologist believes I have Long COVID and I'm handling it as well as anyone knows how to handle it.

I won't put you through the details but days after I see the pulmonologist, the ugly, two-month ordeal of the tooth begins. COVID seeks out and exploits every weakness in the body. There has been an epidemic of broken teeth throughout the pandemic. I'm sure I've been clenching my jaw and that would be my weakest, most vulnerable tooth. Still, dentist, periodontist, and oral surgeon agree — in my case, the teeth show no evidence of bruxism. But of the seven people I know with Long COVID, three of us have lost teeth over the last months. What can be said for sure is my tooth was cracked, it required an oral surgeon to remove it, and getting to the point of getting in to see the surgeon took weeks, weeks in which I developed a dangerous infection. There were two incidences of me lying on the floor weeping while pleading on the phone with receptionists as I begged for help. This consumed the holiday period from Thanksgiving until well past Christmas. Two rounds of debilitating antibiotics to fight infection, bone chips emerging through the gums, the surgical site reopened to flush and remove fragments.

January and February I spent recuperating from the tooth event. As I approached the one-year mark since onset of COVID symptoms, Kent Taylor, CEO of the Texas Roadhouse restaurant chain, committed suicide at age sixty-five after what his family described as a "battle with post-COVID related symptoms, including severe tinnitus." Taylor was one of the good guys, a CEO who when the pandemic hit chose to forego his own salary and bonuses so the money could be used to support frontline, hourly workers. As someone who has always loved to be free of the noise of human activity, and to spend long hours in the quiet of the mind, the relentless, inescapable ringing of the tinnitus COVID has left me with can be very difficult to bear. I do my best to distract myself, I play sleep music all night long, and I tell myself ridiculous fantasies that I repeat anyway because inexplicably they provide a tiny measure of comfort: to wit, I tell myself the tinnitus is like the sound of the ocean in a nautilus shell, that it's the whisper and support of ancestors in the whorl of my own ears. But I completely understand Kent Taylor. Even as I feel for his family.

❖

We cannot live in the relentlessness of our culpability and our complicity. We need respite and resolutions. At the least, some steps in the direction of health. Something I knew before the pandemic that became a lifeline during it.

❖

Living in a rural area, the automobile is our most egregious contribution to global warming but we do work to offset that by keeping nearly half of our 120 acres in woodland, trees that gobble carbon dioxide and particulates out of the air. According to the carbon footprint calculators one can find online, our trees are offsetting our carbon footprints and then some by a wide margin, even when applied to our electricity usage and occasional plane trip, in addition to the fossil fuels consumed by our vehicles.

We raise much of our own food, and given area rainfall here compared with rainfall in the country's most productive food-producing areas, the labor we put into gardening contributes to reductions in both irrigation and transportation of goods. Our eggs, and sometimes our meat, are locally sourced.

For some forty years, we heated with wood and cooled by opening the windows. Fuel for the woodstove was first supplied by trees my husband, his father, and our friend, Fred, harvested from our own farm. We did drag the logs out of the woods with a tractor not horse power but very little fossil fuel was consumed in the process of heating our home. As we got busy with other projects (and as we aged), Steve began purchasing logs from local loggers, pretty much all of whom had been one-time students of Steve's when he taught high school wood shop.

Heating with wood is labor intensive and without nuance: you split the wood, stack the wood, transfer the wood into the house, and then feed the tree chunks into the firebrick-lined wood furnace with its catalytic converter. When you manually feed a fire in the cellar instead of turning up a thermostat, you are keenly aware of just what sort of beast you have brought into your home. Care and feeding of the fire are constantly on your radar during the cold weather months.

Our house is a Cape, a centuries-old design that presumes wood heat. The core of rising heat funneling up the central staircases served us well for decades. In recent years though, we took advantage of state and federal incentives to install a geothermal unit that provides both heating and cooling. The pump and fan to produce and circulate the geothermal have raised our electric bill some, but on the other hand, there are the wind turbines that are sprouting to the northeast of us along the ridgeline of Tuscarora. The electricity the Bluestone Wind Farm will produce when the turbines are activated later this year is expected to be enough to power our whole county, and then some.

❖

According to the U.S. Energy Information Administration, prior to 2006, few wind turbines installed in the US were as tall as 80 meters. Between 2006 and 2012, the average height of new installations rose to that 80 meters mark, and according to Energy.gov, the website of the federal Department of Energy, by 2022, the height of utility-scale land-based wind turbines had increased rapidly to an average of 98 meters. Northlands Power, the project's owner, reports that the twenty-six turbines being built and installed for Bluestone on the ridge in sight of our house are 120 meters high, significantly above average — roughly equivalent to a thirty-six-story building rising out of the woodland. The energy those turbines will produce will go into the grid, and while Northlands touts that can power the whole county, no one believes those turbines are being built to power Broome County. Admirably, a significant proportion of Broome County's energy needs are already being supplied by methane recovered at the Broome County Landfill through our landfill gas (LFG) collection system and the LFG-to-energy facility. If needed, yes, power from the Bluestone turbines will be used here but the principal reason for these giant turbines lies elsewhere. Elsewhere in the state, and most especially downstate in New York City.

Who decides where to site projects? Can one share a goal of clean, renewable energy and yet have concerns about the best place to site projects? As the Brookings Institute has pointed out, "Even though people like wind and solar power in the abstract, some object to large projects near their homes, especially if they don't financially benefit from the project. Transmission for renewable power can also be unpopular, and even more difficult to site when the power is just passing through an area, rather than directly benefiting local residents." New York State has established a target for the state of 70 percent of the state's electricity coming from renewable sources by 2030. When that law was passed in 2019, siting boards were required to include two residents from a community affected by a project, but within months of setting that target, another law passed that abolished those boards and established in their place a new state agency, the Office of Renewable Energy Siting that is now in charge of ruling on renewable energy applications. The proviso to include residents from affected communities no longer applies. The law is intended to fast track green energy projects and it delights many environmentalists but is a source of much concern to many upstate communities.

In addition to state targets, New York City itself has committed to moving to 100 percent "clean and renewable" energy for city government operations by 2025. The NYC Mayor's Office of Climate and Environmental Justice points out on their webpage that "NYC uses about the same amount of electricity as the entire state of Massachusetts but has only 1/35 the space! There is simply not enough room to generate all the clean energy we need while relying only on space within the crowded five boroughs. To meet our 100% clean energy goal while satisfying NYC's electricity demands, we will need to build new transmission lines to bring clean energy into NYC." Meeting the needs of New York City from outside the five boroughs is an issue capable of producing considerable friction. The Mayor's Office of Climate and Environmental Justice points out that the infrastructure projects to power New York City with wind, solar, and hydropower will come from upstate New York and Canada. To those of us living in the rural areas that already supply New York City's water, much of their food, and where tractor-trailer trucks loaded with their garbage motor over our local roads at all hours of the day or night 365 days a year, there is a wariness about who will bear the collateral costs of New York City's appetites.

By the time most Windsor and Sanford residents learned of the proposed siting of the Bluestone Wind project, leases had already been signed with some of the landowners, all of which included nondisclosure clauses legally preventing the landowners from discussing the leases or their terms. Once the proposal became more widely known, an organization of concerned citizens sprang up but their efforts were futile.

NIMBY — not in my back yard — is a predictable reaction to large-scale development projects such as this and as the history of the New York City water supply suggests, relations between the New York City metropolitan area and the rest of the state are often fractious. Just as Midwest and Western states who benefit from a much larger share of federal funds than what they contribute seldom factor that in when objecting to what they see as interference from "Washington," upstaters typically don't focus on any statewide benefits attributable to having New York City as a part of the state when the NYC voting bloc enforces plans advantageous to the city but disadvantageous to rural state residents living hours (and worlds) away. Area residents here who fought the Bluestone Wind project were often in favor of alternative energy, but opposed to the siting process. If the major beneficiary of the Bluestone turbines will be NYC, and NYC already owns thousands of acres twenty miles away at Cannonsville, a site also located on ridges, along a major river system, why, wondered many Windsor and Sanford residents, were the turbines not sited on NYC-owned land around Cannonsville, where homes, farms, and towns have already been obliterated to fulfill the needs of New York City?

Politics and who benefits financially will always factor into, and complicate, all societal efforts to reverse and mitigate what we have done and are doing to the earth. It is unproductive to think otherwise and, in our area, motivations such as those are generally presumed to be the reasons why Bluestone is in our valley, not on Cannonsville land but my bit of research into the history of the New York water supply suggests a different reason. A not-unrelated reason, but, significant, and from the City point-of-view, practical.

The fact that looms large for those charged with administering the NYC water supply but that is not often discussed in the wider community, perhaps because it's the definition of a political football, is that New York City enjoys an exceptional water supply serving 8.5 million City residents and nearly 1 million residents of Westchester, Putnam, Orange, and Ulster counties, yet has no water filtration system. None. Were New York City forced to build a water filtration plant, the aforementioned Riverkeeper organization estimates costs for construction to be at $8 billion to $12 billion, with operating costs of $350 million annually. That is the rationale behind the huge acreage surrounding the reservoirs — the city took by eminent domain not only the acreage under the water, but all the surrounding area that drains into those lakes — the reservoirs plus their watersheds. I never heard any official point this out to our area residents protesting the siting, but the Bluestone Windfarm could not be sited on Cannonsville land that New York City owns because nothing can happen on the lands surrounding those reservoirs that can in any way endanger the quality of the water.

Officials don't bring it up, perhaps because it would quickly devolve into battles of who pays and who benefits but the sacrosanct set-aside nature of those vast tracts of upstate is an ongoing source of discontent for nearby residents. In his *New York Times* review of Lucy Sante's *Nineteen Reservoirs: On Their Creation and the Promise of Water for New York City*, Dwight Garner points to Sante's observation that "[the artificial lakes are] frustrating for the nearby residents . . . because they are impossibly inviting 'on a hot day in a region with no real lakes, albeit as taboo for swimming or boating as if they were meant for the gods alone.'" The sidewalk hosing, lawn watering, infrastructure leaking, and absolutely-no-trespassing injunctions can feel to upstaters like arrogance and indifference on the part of downstate.

Dating back to the spontaneous brain bleed in my early fifties, I had become far more circumspect about which horses I would climb aboard and now as I worked toward recovery from the Long COVID, the negotiation was between regaining a sense of myself by getting back in the saddle, and taking every reasonable precaution. Gradually through the summer and fall, my sessions with Castle had lengthened to approximate something like a session in the old days. We were not progressing in Castle's training — he was in a holding pattern — but I was progressing in strength and stamina while enormously enjoying being in the saddle, feeling for the time back in my own life. Shadowing what I had done in the winter months before falling sick, that winter we boarded Castle at a friend's barn where I would have access to an indoor arena to ride through the winter months. Castle was a prince — patient, willing, and steady, even the day a fox pursued a rabbit into the kickboards that lined the indoor arena. Hidden from view, a blood-curdling life-and-death struggle ensued with screams from both the hunter and the hunted. Few horses I have ever known could have handled it better than what Castle did.

He was home again as I reached the one-year mark and we went on with our sessions in our own familiar outdoor riding ring overlooking the valley.

❖

As a nation we have long lived the self-serving narrative of national identity spun out of a combination of the pious parochialism of the Puritans and the tissue of fabrication John Smith invented to suggest that European dominance of the Americas was (1) God's plan; and (2) at base a love story where Europe was the enterprising and valorous male that America, the fecund and welcoming female, was fortunate to have caught the favor of, a high-minded mirage language has managed to massage and largely keep whole for centuries now because the tale has served the needs of the powerful. Viewed from far enough away, one could consider it ironic that fabricated narratives are exactly what most threaten both the future of the American system of politics, and on a larger scale, threaten the life of our species (and so many other species) here on this planet.

What I remember is the sensation of being launched, and the conviction that I was not going to be able to stop what came next, a realization that took me by surprise as it had been years since I had come off of a horse. Castle and I were at the tail end of a pleasant and unremarkable session in which we had already accomplished the customary walk, trot, canter, a bit of lateral work and were now moseying along considering whether or not there was time for a meander about the pasture to finish things off. Both horse and rider were relaxed, unconcerned. Mid-June and admittedly wildflowers, especially the daisy bugbane, were tall at the edges of the ring. I mention that detail since our only explanation for Castle's unlooked-for eruption was that he must have brushed against and irritated a pollinator and much as you or I would do if we were stung by a bee or wasp we hadn't even noticed, he startled and leapt. The first unexpected buck unseated me just enough that the second sent me headfirst over the horse's shoulder, diving into the hard dirt.

To my good fortune, Stephen was right there in the ring with me. Initially the fall looked minor to him; he expected me to hop up and dust myself off ruefully. But instead, I lay still. Confused, the horse stayed by me for a moment or two and then wandered over to the open gate, looking back at Stephen crouched over me, never venturing up to the barn with his friends. No one had ever come off of him before and Castle clearly seemed to have in mind that he was still supposed to be working and he waited there for further instructions. There could be no clearer demonstration that he was as shocked as any of us by the drama that was unfolding.

We're at the point in our lives where famous people who are younger than we are now die and you can tell from the way that the commentators talk about the lost notable that they think he or she has lived a full life, had their allotment. It stings to hear that. Are we in the October of our lives, as we dearly hope, or is it already November? December even . . .

December

The waxing moon this month had snow cover to radiate against, an atmosphere of chill brilliance. With a day of rain and one more day of mild temperatures though, the grass re-reveals, the horses exuberant in their daily turnout. Nightfall and now the full moon is a round white O of appraisal, potent pout perusing the night long, as to just what we've come to.

Though my passion for horses seems to have been innate, my access to horses initially came principally through lessons at college, lessons for which the insurance company required helmets. They require helmets because statistically one is more likely to sustain a traumatic brain injury from horseback riding than from football, boxing, skiing, diving into lakes, etcetera. I note that most of these equestrian accidents they're counting do not result in death or permanent disability — aquatic sports and roller sports such as skateboarding have a lower total number of incidents than equestrian sports but the poorest record of all sports on the severity of the injury. Still, the evidence for risk associated with equestrian activities is such that a condition of the facility's insurance is very often the reason why lesson stables, dude ranches, and riding adventure providers keep a tack room full of helmets in various sizes and require you to wear one.

Compliance among those not being prodded by a condition of their insurance can look quite different — lore and knowledge about horse care and riding are often passed down generation to generation and old habits can be hard to alter — but because my own access to horses didn't begin until I was eighteen and unfolded through formal lessons, I never had the habit of riding bare-headed and never found the helmets burdensome. Ironically over the last fifty-some years that I have been riding, the only time I would ride helmetless would be in the show ring where science still has not successfully replaced tradition and riders present their horses in high-stress situations wearing top hats, derbies, and Stetsons depending on their division — head coverings made out of cloth and intended for fashion not protection. But at home, the warm-up areas on the show grounds, anywhere but the show ring, I have always had the helmet on. Blessedly, I had one on that day.

Bless as well cell phones, and the two off-duty EMTs who were former students of Stephen's who heard the call, realized it was us, and rushed over to stay with Stephen through the wait for the ambulance. Stephen has informed me that I kept telling the attendants to be careful as they lifted and loaded me into the ambulance but I have no memory of that. I woke briefly in the ambulance as they labored to get an IV line in but I don't remember arriving at the hospital, the CAT scan, the X-rays. I do remember the voice of the surgeon telling me, "I'm Dr. S., you are bleeding in your brain and I have to operate immediately." I felt an unruffled acceptance of this news. It was clear to me some kind of drastic measure was in order and meanwhile the whole of my body was so focused on staying alive that no energy remained for speculation or anxiety.

And then I remember waking in the ICU. Waking, and gradually realizing that it was a remarkable thing that I knew who I was, where I was, why I was there. I woke up cognitively intact. For whatever remains of my life, any complaint the future may visit upon me must be tempered by the fact that I woke up from brain surgery. And I woke up as me.

It was six days in the ICU, then two full weeks in the rehab hospital. For the first week you're euphoric you have lived but gradually the reality of recovery sets in. I know exactly how lucky I am. I was signed off of speech therapy during my initial evaluation session, where I indulged in a bit of showing off. Not content with merely retelling the little narratives the therapist read to me, I would first retell it step-by-step as presented, and then outline how I thought the story could be improved if they had only changed it this way or that. It seemed to me my brain was working well, but I couldn't help but worry a bit that I might be thinking that only because I was in fact damaged and so I was pushing hard for a performance of "I'm fine" in the hopes I could get professionals to confirm for me that I was as close to fine as anyone could expect in that circumstance.

Not infrequently still I find it hard to believe a surgeon actually peeled back a horseshoe of skin from my scalp, drilled through my skull, and vacuumed a blood clot out of my brain. That I had experienced a trauma was easy to believe. With all the broken bones — both hands, four ribs, and the right scapula — I was reduced to being unable to do anything on my own, but the pain meds kept things adequately in bounds and within my brain I felt intact — more intact than I had felt during the worst of Long COVID — making the notion of having had your head opened up feel surreal. Once I got out of ICU and had a bathroom mirror to look in, I could see my half-shaved head and the long line of scabbed-over staples so I knew the rumor to be true, but that doesn't mean it wasn't, and isn't still, difficult to accept.

In the rehab hospital, fulfilling your four therapy appointments — two each of physical therapy and occupational therapy — plus going for as many walks in the hospital hallways as I can persuade an aide to take me on, and then resting in the recliner, napping even, felt like a victorious day. The chart of life expectancy according to birth year informs me that I have already outlived my expiration date but the trauma doctor in charge of my care at the rehab hospital tells me I'm a young woman with an old birth certificate and it's that I choose to listen to.

I am hungry to feel competent and accomplished but once home, in the face of my old life and all the tasks I can see around me, how hard it is to convince myself that increased stamina, longer walks (with someone to hold you by the transfer belt), more agile stair climbing equate to accomplishment.

Seven weeks after the accident, with the neurosurgeon's blessing, we go to Cape Cod for a week in a house we rent with our two children and four grandchildren in Popponesset. What a gift that is. Here at the beach community I've been coming to since I was a toddler, I am walking into the balm of happy memories and the sweet susurration of the surf. I can *be,* rather than needing to *be accomplished.* Incredibly therapeutic. I take my first solo walk on the flat, sea-level streets there in Popponesset.

Back home, ten weeks past the accident, I find myself discouraged about the deficits I presumed would have corrected themselves by now — the spot in the left eye, the lingering dizziness and fatigue, the hives. On the one hand, I'm alive. On the other hand, why do the risk takers all around me — the helmetless bicyclists, the weaving-through-traffic motorcyclists on crotch rockets, the friends we know to be vaccine-free dining inside restaurants — seem to suffer no consequences, while despite my caution and attentiveness, I have walloped my brain and damaged my body? I remind myself of the multiple people I know as deserving as I whose unlooked-for condition means they would gladly trade with me. Our presumption that life should be fair has always been false and I've known that viscerally at least since my mother's sudden death from pneumonia when I was fifteen, but seemingly, the desire for life to have some semblance of fairness is a nearly ineradicable urge.

With the deep instinct for survival, the human animal craves oxygen, water, sleep, nourishment, and — and this is the one that distinguishes us from other animals, and the one that most endangers us and other species — anything that will bolster our sense of self-worth. Bolstering our sense of self-worth can range from the noble (seeking a cure for cancer or an avenue that can alleviate poverty) to the pernicious and therein lies the danger — humans will defend crap, even when we know it to be crap, with the last ounce of our strength if we perceive the crap as vital to our sense of ourselves as worthwhile. When our self-worth is at stake, we are stupendously agile at self-delusion. Thus, the Pilgrims create a narrative wherein God has rained down plague on the indigenous people of the Americas in order to make room for them — mass death becomes a welcome-in message direct from God — and this plotline of colonization as a mission from God powers more than just that band of religious zealots. Simultaneously Europe embraces John Smith's version of this collision of worlds as being at base a love story where Europe is the enterprising and valorous male that America, the fecund and welcoming female, should consider herself fortunate to have caught the favor of. Both of these high-minded mirages we have formulated into the origin stories of our national identity, through the magic of language, the prodigious instrument of the imagination, which has allowed us down through the centuries to massage and largely keep whole these stories that have so ably served the egos and ambitions of the . . . well, I started to say, the elite but that's a category that of late has been so misassigned and denigrated as to be approaching meaninglessness. These narratives of national identity have allowed the successful to attribute their success to merit and virtue with no nagging worries that inequality of opportunity and/ or egregious surfeit might have a role.

The present divisiveness in American politics and culture is a protean struggle over narratives of national identity, and much as was true in the seventeenth century, is a contest that engages deeply in the philosophical question of the nature of truth. What does it mean to be an American? and what is the nature of truth? are inextricably linked questions. It is language and the human imagination that create both national identity, and beyond national identity, the larger notions of truth and falsehood. The difference between now and then is significant however.

While spin has ever been a feature of social constructions everywhere, in recent years in the United States, spin has spun out into overt constructions of alternate realities. Writing in the summer of 2022 (August 3), Heather Cox Richardson in her *Letters from an American* succinctly notes: "The construction of a world based on lies is a key component of authoritarians' takeover of democratic societies. George Orwell's *1984* explored a world in which those in power use language to replace reality, shaping the past and people's daily experiences to cement their control. They are constantly reconstructing the past to justify their actions in the present." Richardson goes on to point out that Hannah Arendt, the twentieth-century German-Jewish political philosopher best known for her studies of the nature of power and evil, went further, saying that the lies of an authoritarian were designed not to persuade people, but to organize them into a mass movement. Followers would "believe everything and nothing," Arendt wrote, "think that everything was possible and that nothing was true." "The ideal subject" for such a dictator, Arendt wrote, was not those who were committed to an ideology, but rather "people for whom the distinction between fact and fiction . . . and the distinction between true and false . . . no longer exist." Richardson then reminds us of the October 2004 *New York Times* article about the presidency of George W. Bush by journalist Ron Suskind, in which Suskind quotes "a senior advisor to Bush" (believed by many to have been Karl Rove) as saying that people like the journalist were in "the reality-based community," which he defined as people who "believe solutions emerge from your judicious study of discernible reality." The aide who might or might not have been Rove went on to say, "That's not the way the world really works anymore. . . . We are an empire now, and when we act, we create our own reality. And while you're studying that reality — judiciously, as you will — we'll act again, creating other new realities, which you can study too, and that's how things will sort out. We're history's actors . . . and you, all of you, will be left to just study what we do." A perceptive observation but, particularly if the speaker was indeed Rove, he seems not to have envisioned quite how fully the impulse for the powerful to create their own reality can go. A decade and a half after the remark Suskind had reported on, Rove himself wrote a blistering editorial printed in the *Wall Street Journal* on the first anniversary of the notorious January 6 assault on the capital, decrying the near-wholesale embrace by the Republican Party of the narrative of an unfair election, a narrative they know without a doubt to be a lie.

In addition to the pollution of domestic politics by one party's complete abandonment of any pretense of trying for the truth over a self-serving narrative, we have the evidence our security units have repeatedly brought us demonstrating that language propagated by the authoritarian Putin regime in Russia (a prime actor though not the sole actor), amplified by social media, and designed to weaken Western democracy has had and is having a measurable effect on American politics and society. Many would say Putin's disinformation campaign has done more to undermine Western democracy than Russia's (and its Soviet predecessor's) entire costly arsenal of nuclear weapons has done. The power of words.

Horse people always ask other horse people about the gory details of any accident. We might be tactful enough to wait some time before asking, but we know we are dealing with animals that don't have to mean to hurt you to damage you irreparably and so we want the details as a cautionary tale.

Twenty-three years before my traumatic brain injury, Maxine Kumin was involved in a carriage accident that broke her neck, among other serious injuries. The first time I saw Max at her farm after her recovery, we did not go for the usual walk up to the garden, past the pond, along the lovely carriage trails they had built through the woods. That visit without the walk is the time we talked about the accident, the day she said to herself in my presence, *hubris*.

Deuteronomy was a homebred — a grandson of the mare that Maxine had rescued so long ago, who had the unnerving habit of running away. But Deuter, the grandson, had been carefully and knowledgably bred and brought along and had never been subjected to the bad experiences that had made his grand-dam unreliable. The whole point to the clinic at the Green Mountain Horse Association facility in South Woodstock, Vermont, that day was to continue the education of horse and driver, and to give Deuter mileage in a controlled environment.

Combined driving events test the horses and drivers in three separate areas. The marathon phase of the competition is fast enough and grueling enough that you need a special carriage manufactured of steel, aluminum, or other alloys to stand up to the beating it will take on the cross-country terrain you will encounter. You don't want to have any cart dragged over you but you particularly don't want a metal marathon cart pulled over you.

That summer day Deuter was hitched to the marathon cart with Max at the lines and they were just driving around a grassy area warming up when she heard the cry "loose horse" and a panicked Fjord horse bolted by, spooking Deuter.

There's getting on and there is not getting on. Whether riding or driving a horse, it is that black and white. Once you've committed to getting on, then the safest response to almost any emergency is to ride (or drive) on. You don't get to just get off. You have to keep your head, send them forward, reassure them, bring them back to you. Which is exactly what Max did. She kept her wits and drove through the problem. By her account to me she was justifiably feeling pretty good about herself and her horse. The Fjord was caught up and she had maneuvered Deuter, still tense and worried but back in hand, over toward the edge of the field away from the commotion. It was in her moment of relief that the empty logging truck came up behind her, barreling down the dirt road bordering the GMHA property, its slack chain sides swaying and clanging. Her horse came momentarily unglued. But a moment is all it takes. The carriage overturned in Deuter's desperate bound sideways, Max was spilled to the ground and the heavy metal contraption dragged right over the top of her.

One of the people on the grounds that day was a nurse. Heroically she held Max's head still and talked her through the long, long wait for the medevac helicopter. By what miracle did they get her into the helicopter and then into the trauma center without damaging the spinal cord? Ninety-five percent of the people who sustain the vertebral fractures Maxine sustained die of their injuries; 95 percent of those who survive never walk again. With the love and support of her family and her own adamantine will, Maxine both lived and walked. Never again to be as supple, never again to be without pain, but she knew full well how lucky she was.

In the fifteen-plus years that came after the accident, Max had plenty of time to contemplate and second guess her judgment in still participating in horse sports at that level and thus there were days when the ongoing pain would cause her to castigate herself for hubris, for being out there that day. It's a warning that deserves serious consideration. But to me — and I think and hope for Max at many other times — the fact that she and Deuter got through the first emergency proves her skills and judgment were sound. Whatever our age, we need some luck. The good fortune not to have emergencies pile on top of one another. In the risk-benefit analysis, how much bad luck can one plan for? My neurosurgeon has said the decision is up to me — only I can make the determination of how the scales balance between risk and passion. But, yes, insults to the brain are cumulative. I hear Max's rueful *hubris*.

For the tennis player or the golfer, when to quit can be left up to the body to decide with much less risk and much more clarity. With horses, our partner in the enterprise can get you in deeper than the body might have the reflexes and strength to get you out of. But simultaneously the horse is a living being with a brain of its own that can sometimes override your folly.

Did you ever know a three-legged dog? I once knew a beagle named Jock who had lost a front leg, an energetic little tricycle of a dog. The directness, the joie de vivre even, with which he accepted what was left of his life and got on with it, unabashedly dedicating himself to every moment from dinner bowl to squirrel patrol to frisbee play to naps in the sunshine. Those of us coming out of some long period of recovery need to learn to recognize that today, now, this may well be it, this may well be as full as recovery will ever be, and abandon ourselves to it, wring every modicum of joy from each moment with the insouciance and aplomb of a three-legged dog.

What is termed "Early American Literature" focuses on the colonial period up through the early national period, a centuries-long period in which those "practical Americans" produced very little in the way of imaginative writing that we commonly associate with the term *literature*. Journals, diaries, letters, sermons, captivity narratives, political broadsides, and speeches make up the canon of Early American Literature. When I taught this period, two texts I often paired together were John Winthrop's sermon *A Modell of Christian Charity* and Roger Williams's January 1655 *Letter to Providence*.

In the wake of the Pilgrims founding of Plymouth in 1620, in 1630 John Winthrop led the first wave of settlers to form Massachusetts Bay Colony, the settlement that became Boston. Subsequently, Roger Williams was expelled from Massachusetts Bay in 1636, for espousing two unpopular opinions. The first of the radical causes Williams advocated for was the idea that land should not just be confiscated from the Native Americans, that it needed to be negotiated and paid for since the land was theirs. Roger Williams's second dangerous opinion centered on his ideas for the political organization of community, revolutionary ideas that directly competed with the plan outlined by Winthrop and the bulk of the other Puritans.

There's some disagreement among scholars as to whether Winthrop delivered his *A Modell of Christian Charity* sermon to the assembled settlers before they embarked on their voyage, or onboard ship just before disembarking in Massachusetts. Either way, this is the moment in American history when the Jewish narrative of a chosen people gets applied to a little band of religiously motivated settlers who are facing a hard task. In *On Christian Charity*, Winthrop gave voice to words that have echoed down through our history, the ringing source material for the American sense of our exceptionalism: *wee shall be as a city upon a hill* — a light to the world — *the eyes of all people are uppon us*. It's a revelation to the students to realize that in context, those words are no "we're number one" boast; rather they are a promise and a warning: "[God] hath taken us to be his, after a most strickt and peculiar manner which will make him the more jealous of our love and obedience."

Winthrop is rallying and remonstrating, laying out their mission, their obligations to God and to one another, and a vision of ideal community that he understands as God-given. He opens with his understanding of that God-given model on which he is basing the community they are being called to form: "God Almighty in his most holy and wise providence hath soe disposed of the condition of mankind as in all times some must be rich, some poore, some high and eminent in power and dignitie, others mean and in submission."

Yes, he takes as his given that God made lions mighty and mosquitoes not and that therefore that meant that it was God's intention that some people should be eminent and some in subjugation. If this is God's plan, it is useless to rail against that order, but he recognizes if you are not one of those graced with eminence in power and dignity that you might chafe against this so he immediately assembles "the reason hereof," which Winthrop sees as threefold: (1) this will "hold conformity with the rest of his world" (this is the "variety and difference of the Creatures" I have already referred to); (2) this variety of humanity gives God room to manifest the variety of his powers; and the penultimate reason for his purposes; (3) So that we humans would need one another and would bond together in community.

Winthrop sees them as being called to fulfill the Corpus Christi model of community first described by the apostle Paul in his letters to the Corinthians — the idea that the people of God are the body of Christ (the corpus Christi), each with their ordained role, all working together and bound together by love.

Since this love is the glue holding his community together, "the bond of perfection" in his phrasing, Winthrop does address the question of the source of this love. The answer Winthrop says is "Simile simili gaudet or like will to like ... This is the cause why the Lord loves the Creature [the Creature here being humans], soe farre as it hathe any of his Image in it, he loves his elect because they are like himselfe ... So a mother loves her childe, because shee thoroughly conceives a resemblance of herselfe in it."

In the hierarchy of importance Winthrop is delineating, there is a "we" specially chosen by God for this mission of founding America, and a host of "thems" who are outside this special covenant. History gives us a pretty clear idea how people for whom no resemblance to the self can be worked out are treated. Even one of their own like Roger Williams or Anne Hutchison could be turned out into the New England winter for failing to adequately reflect resemblance to the established order.

I'm wrapping up on Winthrop's vision here but one more essential piece: having laid out his model of a community, the question remains, if human community is to work together as a single body, who gets to be the brain? For his group, the question is rhetorical. God is the obvious answer but how do we know what God wants? The men upon whom God's favor has been manifested by their having been chosen for eminence and power are the representatives of God on earth. Winthrop does not feel the need to express that explicitly, but he does make clear that they have come to Massachusetts "to seeke out a place of cohabitation and Consorteshipp under a due forme of Government both civill and ecclesiasticall," which is to say church and state authority shall be one.

By contrast, Roger Williams was arguing for all members of his community to have "liberty of conscience." Williams believed firmly that the state should not come between him and his God, and furthermore he understood that for him to have that freedom, it was a freedom that must be extended to everyone. Williams was advocating for separation of church and state not to protect the state from the church but to protect the individual's faith, whatever that faith might be, from the state.

Granting that the Narragansetts might not have traditionally shared English notions of land ownership, that didn't mean that they didn't comprehend how European contact was remaking their world. They were very clear on the difference between the bulk of Puritans who interpreted "The Great Dying," the pandemics among the indigenous populations that contact caused, as God clearing out the place so they could take possession, and this anomalous figure, Roger Williams, who understood himself as moving into someone else's territory and thus as morally obligated to negotiate mutually beneficial and agreeable terms. When Williams was expelled by his fellow Puritans, the Narragansetts sold him the land on which he began Providence Plantations, plantation then being a term that referred to colonies. Williams did not apply to the English crown for permission to begin his colony because he believed the English had no legitimate claim to Wampanoag and Narragansett territory. He did finally petition Charles I for a colonial patent in 1643, only because he wanted to officially combine the settlements of Providence, Newport, and Portsmouth (Portsmouth being the area he had helped Ann Hutchison to purchase from the Narragansetts when she also was expelled by the Puritans for heresy), to protect those communities against incursions from Plymouth and Massachusetts Bay, which had been trying to exploit Hutchison's and Williams's lack of a patent. Although

England was in the midst of its Civil War at the time, Williams did manage to get the patent from Parliament.

During the two months it took for Roger Williams to sail to England to arrange the patent, he authored *A Key into the Language of America*, which is a dictionary of indigenous languages, principally Narragansett, an Algonquin language, interspersed with Williams's observations of indigenous cultures, often presented as superior to elements of European culture. Some of the words introduced into English by Williams's *Key* include *moose, moccasin, squash, powwow, quahog,* and *succotash*. Fascinating as I find the text, it is not the *Key* that I would have students read in my class, but rather his "To the Town of Providence" letter (January 1655), written to settle a controversy over just how far this freedom of conscience he espoused should extend — where is the dividing line that keeps liberty of conscience from becoming an anarchical community? In this letter Williams affirms that he never advocated "infinite Liberty of Conscience," and that a civil government needs the power to enforce civil obedience. To prevent misunderstandings, Williams proposes a metaphor. Whereas Winthrop had described the ideal of their community as a body where God (in the person of the magistrates and ministers) was the brain and had ordained the role in this body for each, a role that was to be accepted and adhered to, by contrast Williams's metaphor for community was a ship at sea.

> It hath fallen out sometimes, that both papists and protestants, Jews, or Turks, may be embarked in one ship; upon which supposal I affirm, that all the liberty of conscience, that ever I pleaded for, turns upon these two hinges — that none of the papists, protestants, Jews, or Turks, be forced to come to the ships prayers of worship, nor compelled from their own particular prayers or worship, if they practice any. I further add, that I never denied, that notwithstanding this liberty, the commander of this ship ought to command the ship's course; yea, and also command that justice, peace, and sobriety, be kept and practiced, both among the seamen and all the passengers.

No government should come between any conscience and that individual's understanding (or lack thereof) of a divine presence, yet that civil government has every right to hold members to such laws of civil government as to promote justice and peace. Williams's very metaphor also implies a more mobile society than the one envisioned by Winthrop. No toe will ever become a right hand but a cabin boy (or a passenger) could one day become captain.

Religious liberty and consent of the governed to an extraordinary degree had been written into the Rhode Island charter. In the wake of the 1643 patent, discontents and disagreements led Williams, along with John Clarke of Newport, to travel back to England in 1651. Parliamentary forces had executed Charles I in 1649, and in the turmoil a charter for Rhode Island was not a high priority. Williams went back to Providence in 1654, but Clarke stayed on to continue pursuing a charter. After years of hard work, and after the restoration of King Charles II, in July of 1663, Clarke succeeded in obtaining a Royal Charter, which afforded unprecedented religious freedom, and included the right to elect their own governor rather than having one appointed by the monarchy. The Charter called this "a lively experiment."

Rhode Island was the last of the states to ratify the US Constitution, and it was so because its citizens insisted on the Bill of Rights, in particular their precious freedom of religion. With pressure mounting from the other states, Rhode Island did finally vote to ratify the Constitution on May 29, 1790, but ratification of the Bill of Rights was still on the table. Newly elected president George Washington, along with his Secretary of State Thomas Jefferson traveled to Newport in August of 1790 to acknowledge gratitude for the ratification vote and to address the concerns of Rhode Islanders.

Business leaders, clergy, and other prominent citizens greeted Washington and his contingent with letters of welcome, including one from Moses Seixas, warden of the Touro Synagogue. The Touro Synagogue of Newport is America's first and oldest Jewish congregation. Seixas's letter asked Washington about his administration's policy toward Jews. A few days after leaving Newport, Washington sent a response addressed "to the Hebrew Congregation in Newport, Rhode Island" that makes clear that the American government Washington pictures and proposes goes beyond mere tolerance.

> The Citizens of the United States of America have a right to applaud themselves for having given to mankind examples of an enlarged and liberal policy: a policy worthy of imitation. All possess alike liberty of conscience and immunities of citizenship. It is now no more that toleration is spoken of, as if it was by the indulgence of one class of people, that another enjoyed the exercise of their inherent natural rights. For happily the Government of the United States, which gives to bigotry no sanction, to persecution no assistance, requires only that they who live under its protection should demean themselves as good citizens.

It is one of many letters Washington wrote to clergy and religious congregations of many persuasions in unqualified support of the First Amendment's guarantee of religious freedom. Those who argue that America's founding fathers established a Christian country based on Christian principles can argue so only by willfully ignoring the incontrovertible evidence of the historical record.

The wind has shaped the fallen snow into a calligraphy of affection for the land, each undulating line an echo.

❖

Whether or not I will ride again remains an open question, even well past the six-month line in the sand my neurosurgeon drew. Passion versus prudence, with the choice up to me. It's unimaginable to me how I would ever survive having to endure another injury and surgery such as this one. And how much luck can I count on? It's the fifth insult this brain has sustained, and triumphed over, but damage is cumulative the surgeon allows. Maybe fifty-two years of reveling in a sport I love should be enough. The doctor who oversaw my case in rehab certainly thought so and made his position clear to me.

I was riding a well-trained horse who trusted me and who I trusted; I was wearing my helmet; I had just purchased a larger mounting block to make mounting and dismounting safer as I aged. How much can one plan for? How old is too old? At 40, or 50, 60, 65, 68, despite the bee sting, couldn't I have ridden through those two bucks and laughed off the incident? Or would the lack of any warning have made me vulnerable at any age? Had the damage from Long COVID factored in?

Any athlete pushes themself enough physically to notice the passage of time with more specificity than those whose lives leave them less attuned to their own bodies: the incremental but noticeable losses of strength, endurance, reaction time. But at the same time, there is that elixir of muscle memory: the horse lifts beneath you into an exquisite canter departure, or sidesteps at a blown leaf and with no need to think about it, you move with him as one and feel again the sensation of wholeness when the chattering self feels hushed, satisfied, and centered within the mortal flesh that houses it. Muscle memory for the athlete is Proust's madeleine, a direct line to the limbic brain, effortlessly and urgently returning us, if only for the moment, to our youthful bodies. For riders, in addition there is the centaur effect. Surely that mythology has a basis in this feeling of two species merged, and for the aging rider, you're extending your own body into the body of a young and agile horse. You're bumping up your athleticism exponentially. It's intoxicating — the allure of how it feels in those moments when riding makes your body feel once again temporarily in sync with the age your mind persists in believing you are. A siren call of prodigious power.

At the moment of solstice, the earth here in northeastern United States is deep in the glitteringly cold darkness, the sky moonless, cut with stars, while we two are cocooned in the warm pod of the automobile, floating home from a celebration, the black woodlots and inky swept-out hayfields interspersed with the cheerful smear and spray of Christmas lights on the houses we pass. Those holiday lights are the vestiges of ancient solstice fires, the bright beseeching fires our distant ancestors built to lure back the waning sun. The after-solstice winter dawn a dawning of yet one more chance a blossoming springtime will be on our horizon.

Millennia on, still we nurse and nurture that flicker, that ember of human hope.

I circled the farm pond on this morning's walk. The farm's eye is shut tight with ice, its lid powdered with stars, dreaming as the new year approaches. In the hard light of winter my shadow is sharp-edged and distinct, an agile figure of suggestive solidity striding companionably beside me, as if some possibility still remains that I could impress however lightly some mark of significance on the earth.

A memoir written late in life has ever been a self-authored elegy, but for centuries to situate that elegy amongst observations of the natural world was to locate one's own mortality within a context of continuity and continuance. Now, to write of the natural world amidst the accelerating destruction of the Anthropocene is to write elegy for the planet itself, a far more profound mourning that negates what comfort one might ever have found in the presumption life would roll on well beyond one's own small allotment. This is an elegy for which one struggles to imagine any future audience for. The only audience is the present. Our only hope is ourselves.

WORKS CITED

While this is a creative work, not a scholarly treatment of history or any other field, portions of this book do engage, in the mode of the personal essay, with certain histories, particularly of places where I have had a long association, and with a number of ideas of others. Whenever the ideas of others, or the interpretations others have made of the historical record or other facts are included, the source of those ideas and interpretations are clearly identified in the narrative. In all other cases, the reading/interpretation is my own. For close to thirty years, I taught courses on American Literature, including the early period, at State University of New York at Binghamton. Over the decades I read extensively in the period, both primary texts and contextual materials. Thoughtful reflection on that reading and the experience of engaging with those texts and ideas with highly competent students at Binghamton means that many of my ideas as expressed here developed over a long period of time. That said, I wanted to provide a short list of relevant sources specifically referred to herein, so that readers with a deeper interest in those topics might have a starting point for their own explorations.

Historical Figures

These historical texts are all in the public domain and available in myriad sources both in books and online. I did use two sources that preserved the spelling of the original historical texts; for the rest, I chose reliable sources that transcribed the centuries-old texts in modern spelling. The specific sources I used for each are the following:

Bradford, William. Quote regarding first Thanksgiving from *On Plimoth Plantation*, quoted in Pilgrim Hall Museum. https://pilgrimhall.org/pdf/TG_What_Happened_in_1621.pdf. Last accessed 8/20/2024.

———. Quote on "good hand of God," quoted in Charles C. Mann. "Native Intelligence," *Smithsonian Magazine*, December 2005. https://www.smithsonianmag.com/history/native-intelligence-109314481/.

Charles, King, II, from a Royal Charter, quoted in "An Official Charter; A 'Lively Experiment,'" where King Charles II recognizes the State of Rhode Island and Providence Plantations, and provides for separation of church and state. https://www.brown.edu/about/history/timeline/official-charter-%E2%80%9Clively-experiment%E2%80%9D. Last accessed 9/8/2024.

Crèvecoeur, J. Hector St. John de. *Letters from an American Farmer*. The Avalon Project: Documents in Law, History and Diplomacy, Yale Law School, Lillian Goldman Law Library. https://avalon.law.yale.edu/subject_menus/letters.asp. Last accessed 8/19/2024.

Smith, John. "The Generall Historie of Virginia, New England, and the Summer Isles." Book III, chapter 2. (Smith as captive at the court of Powhatan in 1608.) *The Heath Anthology of American Literature*, vol. A, 17th ed., edited by Paul Lauter, Richard Yarborough, and John Alberti. Boston: Wadsworth Cengage Learning, 2014, 317–18.

———. "A True Relation of Such Occurrences and Accidents of Noate as Hath Hapned in Virginia." (Smith as captive at the court of Powhatan in 1608.) *The Heath Anthology of American Literature*, vol. A, 1st ed., edited by Paul Lauter, Richard Yarborough, and John Alberti. Boston: Wadsworth Cengage Learning, 2006, 258.

Washington, George. "Letter to the Jews of Newport," quoted in Dr. Jonathan D. Sarna, "George Washington's Correspondence with the Jews of Newport." Brandeis University's Hornstein Jewish Professional Leadership Graduate Program. https://www.brandeis.edu/hornstein/sarna/americanjewishcultureandscholarship/tobigotrynosanction.pdf . Last accessed 8/20/2024.

Williams, Roger. 1655 *Letter to Providence*. *The Founders' Constitution*, vol. 5, Amendment I (Religion), document 6. Chicago, IL: University of Chicago Press, quoted from Anton Phelps Stokes, ed. *Church and State in the United States*. 3 vols. New York: Harper, 1950. http://press-pubs.uchicago.edu/founders/documents/amendI_religions6.html.

Winslow, Edward. *Mort's Relation*. Pilgrim Hall Museum. https://pilgrimhall.org/pdf/TG_What_Happened_in_1621.pdf. Last accessed 8/20/2024.

Winthrop, John. "A Modell of Christian Charity," Hanover Historical Texts Collection, Hanover College, Hanover, IN, from the Collections of the Massachusetts Historical Society (Boston, 1838), 3rd series, 7:31–48. https://history.hanover.edu/texts/winthmod.html.

Contemporary Sources

March, Section 3

Paula Peters's account of the first Thanksgiving from a Wampanoag point of view comes from a special feature she wrote for the *Cape Cod Times*:

Peters, Paula. "A Man without a Tribe: The True Story of Squanto." *Cape Cod Times*. November 19, 2020. https://www.capecodtimes.com/in-depth/news/2020/11/19/tisquantum-squanto-wampanoag-translator-true-story/6261368002/.

I also read pages from Peters's personal website. Her page on the Peabody Museum site, which I last accessed June 4, 2024, is available at https://peabody.harvard.edu/OE-listening-wampanoag-voices-paula-peters

April, Section 2

Arsenault, Kerri. *Mill Town: Reckoning with What Remains* (New York: St. Martin's Press, 2020).

I listened to Arsenault's book in the audio edition. The quote from the 1881 Massachusetts labor report, the quote from Waldo Pettingill, and Arsenault's own comment on why the KKK targeted Franco-Americans all appear in chapter 3 "Connecting with Dot."

May, Section 5

Millay, Edna St. Vincent. "Lament," *Second April* (New York: Mitchell Kennerly, 1921), 72. This poem is in the public domain.

June, Section 3

Ghosh, Amitav. *The Great Derangement: Climate Change and the Unthinkable* (Chicago, IL: University of Chicago Press, 2016), 19–20.

Ghosh quotes Stephen Jay Gould from Gould's *Time's Arrow, Time's Cycle: Myth and Metaphor in the Discovery of Geologic Time* (Cambridge, MA: Harvard University Press, 1987), 173.

July, Section 10

Stout, Ruth. *Gardening without Work* (Emmaus, PA: Rodale Books, 1960).

August, Section 2

Hinman, Marjory Barnum. *Onaquaga: Hub of the Border Wars of the American Revolution in New York State* (Binghamton, NY: published by the author, 1975).

August, Section 4

The life of Jospeh Brant is discussed in this section, and in September, section 7. The general outline of Joseph Brant's life and his role in what unfolded for Onaquaga I had first been exposed to through my interactions with Marge Hinman, and her writings. My readings in preparation for a doctoral field exam in American literature, and for subsequent decades of teaching American literature, including the early period, had added context. In looking to narrate a streamlined version of the major points of the history of how this valley moved from Haudenosaunee hands to the hands of newly minted Americans, in addition to rereading portions of Hinman's *Onaquaga: Hub of the Border Wars*, I have done a certain amount of browsing respectable online history sites to solidify my timelines and to gain a feel for the consensus of opinions as to how things developed. I was careful to include sites from both the point of view of the revolutionary Americans and the indigenous peoples, sites such as the following:

The George Washington Presidential Library of Mount Vernon. https://www.mountvernon.org/library/digitalhistory/digital-encyclopedia/article/joseph-brant/.

National Museum of the American Indian, Education Office. https://americanindian.si.edu/sites/1/files/pdf/education/HaudenosauneeGuide.pdf.

The Native Heritage Project. https://nativeheritageproject.com/2012/04/17/joseph-brant-warrior-statesman-mohawk-leader/.

August, Section 5

Pineda, Irma. Excerpt from essay "On Nature and Life." Translated by Sally Keith. "What Sparks Poetry" feature of the *Poetry Daily* website, February 2022. https://poems.com/features/what-sparks-poetry/irma-pineda-on-nature-and-life/.

September, Section 4

Wohlleben, Peter. *The Hidden Life of Trees: What They Feel, How They Communicate — Discoveries from a Secret World*, translated by Jane Billinghurst (Vancouver, BC: Greystone Books, 1st English Language ed., 8th printing, 2016).

Bridle, Peter. "If We Can Farm Metal from Plants, What Else Can We Learn from Life on Earth?" *Guardian*, April 15, 2022. https://www.theguardian.com/commentisfree/2022/apr/15/farm-metal-from-plants-life-on-earth-climate-breakdown. The article is a precis of the central thesis of his book, *Ways of Being: Animals, Plants, Machines: The Search for a Planetary Intelligence* (New York: Farrar, Straus and Giroux, 2022).

September, Section 8

For readers looking for a definitive history of the New York City Water Supply that includes not only the engineering feat but also the perspectives of the condemned towns and villages, and the workers who built the reservoirs, I recommend Lucy Sante's *Nineteen Reservoirs: On Their Creation and the Promise of Water for New York City*, published late in 2022 by a press called The Experiment, and distributed by Norton. I only recently became aware of this book and did not consult it as a source for my discussion, but I did access the publisher's description as it appears on Sante's website (https://lucysante.com/book/nineteen-reservoirs/), and I quoted from the review of the book in the *New York Times*.

Garner, Dwight, "How New York City Got Its Fresh Water." *New York Times*, August 8, 2022. https://www.nytimes.com/2022/08/08/books/review-nineteen-reservoirs-lucy-sante.html.

To get the timeline, to identify the streams and rivers damned and the towns and villages leveled and flooded for each reservoir, I relied on various online sites such as https://www.nyc.gov/site/dep/water/history-of-new-york-citys-drinking-water.page, https://www.mcny.org/story/contentious-history-supplying-water-manhattan, and others. I also discovered details like the lawsuits brought by the States of Pennsylvania and New Jersey, and the torching of Gilboa by its own residents in several different accounts.

Information on the aging infrastructure of the New York City water supply came from Riverkeeper. https://www.riverkeeper.org/campaigns/safeguard/threats-to-nycs-tap-water/, accessed June 26, 2024.

September, Section 11

Walsh, Bryan "*Why Your Brain Can't Process Climate Change*," *Time magazine*, April 14, 2019. https://time.com/5651393/why-your-brain-cant-process-climate-change/.
McGonigal, Jane. "*Our Puny Human Brains Are Terrible at Thinking about the Future*," *Slate*, April 13, 2017. https://slate.com/technology/2017/04/why-people-are-so-bad-at-thinking-about-the-future.html.

October, Section 3

Brannen, Peter. "The Amazon Is Not Earth's Lungs." *The Atlantic*, August 27, 2019. https://www.theatlantic.com/science/archive/2019/08/amazon-fire-earth-has-plenty-oxygen/596923/?utm_campaign=the-atlantic&utm_content=5d698e93145a5700015359a8_ta&utm_medium=social&utm_source=facebook&fbclid=IwAR3-IP5nk_pgYsafM4suyaU3fLU1Q_UJk_kYCLwzssScgtAaTvX6Xy4TCN4.

October, Section 5

Lenthang, Marlene. "Heartbreaking Photos Show Emaciated Grizzly Bears . . ." *Daily Mail*, October 3, 2019. https://www.dailymail.co.uk/news/article-7532501/Heartbreaking-photos-emaciated-grizzly-bears-Canada-salmon-shortage.html.

As noted, the effects of climate change on salmon and bear are variable — it's the trend that is unmistakable. As update to this 2019 story, the following article refers to September 2023, the most recent autumn to the point at which this book was prepared for press:

McCurry, Justin. "Brown Bear Cubs in Japan Die of Starvation Amid Salmon Shortage." *Guardian*, September 26, 2023. https://www.theguardian.com/world/2023/sep/26/brown-bear-cubs-in-japan-die-of-starvation-amid-salmon-shortage#:~:text=Brown%20bear%20cubs%20in%20Japan%20die%20of%20starvation%20amid%20salmon%20shortage,-This%20article%20is&text=As%20many%20as%20eight%20in,caused%20by%20the%20climate%20crisis.

Troianovski, Anton, and Chris Mooney. "Radical Warming in Siberia Leaves Millions on Unstable Ground." *Washington Post*, October 3, 2019. https://www.washingtonpost.com/graphics/2019/national/climate-environment/climate-change-siberia/.

As I prepared this book for publication, I also rechecked the status of this situation. One example of the continuing concern over this state of the Siberian permafrost would be the following:

Mellen, Ruby and Natalya Saprunova. "Siberia's Ice Is Melting, Revealing Its Past and Endangering Its Future." *Washington Post*, January 3, 2024. https://www.washingtonpost.com/world/interactive/2024/siberia-melting-permafrost-climate-photos/.

October, Section 7

There are many sources that demonstrate that taxes still go to subsidize fossil fuel companies. This is but one example:

Friedman, Lisa. "Zombies of the U.S. Tax Code: Why Fossil Fuels Subsidies Seem Impossible to Kill." *New York Times*, March 15, 2024. https://www.nytimes.com/2024/03/15/climate/tax-breaks-oil-gas-us.html.

October, Section 9

Information on the Colorado River allocation situation and the quote from John Entsminger were taken from an article published in the *Los Angeles Times*, June 14, 2022, written by staff writer, Ian James. https://www.latimes.com/environment/story/2022-06-14/big-water-cutbacks-ordered-amid-colorado-river-shortage.

As I prepared this book for publication, I rechecked the status of the situation; as example I'll note a March 2024 *Los Angeles Times* story written by Lorena Iñiguez Elebee, headlined "We Can Do Better: Western States Are Divided Over Colorado River Plans." https://www.latimes.com/environment/story/2024-03-08/western-states-divided-colorado-river-plans.

November, Section 4

Philip, Marlene NourbeSe. "Meditations on the Declension of Beauty by the Girl with the Flying Cheekbones," from *She Tries Her Tongue, Her Silence Softly Breaks* (Charlottetown, PEI: Ragweed Press, 1969), 52–53.

November, Section 8

Information about average height for wind turbines comes from the federal Energy Information Administration website, https://www.eia.gov/todayinenergy/detail.php?id=33912, and the federal Energy Department's website, https://www.energy.gov/eere/articles/wind-turbines-bigger-better#:~:text=A%20wind%20turbine's%20hub%20height,(~322%20feet)%20in%202022.

Information about the specifics of Northland Power's Bluestone Wind Farm came directly from Northland's website. https://www.northlandpower.com/en/projects-and-updates/bluestone-new-york-onshore-wind.aspx.

Information about the Broome County Landfill's landfill gas system comes from local news reports at the time the facility was being built and state and county documents available online such as https://extapps.dec.ny.gov/data/dar/afs/permits/703990001100004.pdf and https://extapps.dec.ny.gov/data/dar/afs/permits/703990001100004.pdf.

The Brookings Institute report referenced is available at https://www.brookings.edu/articles/renewables-land-use-and-local-opposition-in-the-united-states/.

New York City energy target goals and the quote about the city's energy usage were accessed at https://climate.cityofnewyork.us/subtopics/systems/#:~:text=NYC%20uses%20about%20the%20same,of%20power%20 (NYISO%202022).

The statistics on the number served by New York City Water Supply come from National Institute of Health report. https://www.nyc.gov/assets/dep/downloads/pdf/water/drinking-water/drinking-water-supply-quality-report/2020-drinking-water-supply-quality-report.pdf.

All of the sources in this section were last accessed on June 26, 2024.

December, Section 4

Heather Cox Richardson's Substack *Letters from an American*, August 2, 2022. https://heathercoxrichardson.substack.com/p/august-3-2022?utm_source=publication-search.

Rove, Karl. "Republicans' January 6 Responsibility." *Wall Street Journal*, January 5, 2022. https://www.wsj.com/articles/republicans-jan-6-responsibility-anniversary-riot-storm-capitol-trump-protesters-investigation-11641417707.

December, Section 5

To read more about Maxine Kumin's accident and recovery I refer you to her memoir on the subject:

Kumin, Maxine. *Inside the Halo and Beyond: Anatomy of a Recovery*. New York: W. W. Norton, 2001.

www.ingramcontent.com/pod-product-compliance
Lightning Source LLC
Chambersburg PA
CBHW021157160426
43194CB00007B/785